The CRISIS of HUMAN RIGHTS

Other books by Niels C. Nielsen, Jr.:

Solzhenitsyn's Religion
The Religion of President Carter

The CRISIS of HUMAN RIGHTS

By

Niels C. Nielsen, Jr.

THOMAS NELSON INC., PUBLISHERS
Nashville • New York

Library of Congress Cataloging in Publication Data

Nielsen, Niels Christian, 1921-
   The crisis of human rights.

   Bibliography: p.
   1.   Civil rights.   I.   Title.
JC571.N52   323.4   78–4056
ISBN 0–8407–5644–5

Contents

Preface

Human rights stand at the center of international debate by reason of the sheer urgency of events. Not only is the world divided between East and West, Communist and non-Communist.Newspapers daily bring reports of authoritarian regimes' abuse in non-Communist areas—Africa and South America, for example. Amnesty International won a 1977 Nobel Peace Prize. On humanitarian grounds, it has called attention to arbitrary arrest, torture, and murder—worldwide! In fact, the crisis is felt in virtually every part of the globe. The absence of freedom is recognized by those persons whom the technological revolution is just beginning to affect, as well as by statesmen and intellectuals. President Carter's campaign for human rights, together with debate about the Helsinki agreements, has called attention to the urgency of the crisis.

This book describes selected areas where the situation is most acute. It evaluates issues and conditions from an American Christian perspective. Questions are complex and must be treated at a variety of levels—psychological, philosophical, and theological, as well as political and economic. Overly simplified "answers" are self-defeating in the end. Problems of implementation are international as well as national. The mere announcement of rights does not make them real or effective. Legal and constitutional traditions—the law, the courts, and separation of the judiciary from the executive—provide necessary institutional bases. It is an illusion to suppose that restraint of tyranny and abuse is ever accomplished once and for all!

The crisis of human rights, in the last analysis, is the spiritual crisis of the time. Good intentions alone will not effect change. A "practical" approach is imperative. Attitudes, responses, and results—those that are possible— matter. Yet the question of goals cannot be avoided. Commitment concerning beliefs about human dignity, good and evil, and ultimate reality is not to be discounted. Authoritarian regimes have their ideologies, and they have acquired vast power which they use in blatant disregard of human rights. It is not a coincidence that they attack freedom and religion together.

I believe President Carter has expressed the American consensus—as a kind of Everyman—in his defense of human rights. It would be a mistake to suppose that concern about this issue began or will end with his presidency. Carter has called attention to what is at stake for his nation and the world. At the same time that he affirms the separation of church and state, he recognizes the religious bases of freedom. The problems the Western democracies face are not just in the field of conviction, but of implementation. How can persons—and nations—be motivated to believe in and be dedicated to human rights? In a time of nuclear terror, even more than in the past, personal freedom must be maintained if civilization is not to fall back into barbarism and despair.

Chapter one begins with a survey of the pattern of the crisis in recent years, together with a definition of human rights.

Chapter two considers the role of the Russian dissidents whom the regime is attempting to destroy completely.

Chapter three describes the mounting repression in Czechoslovakia as well as other parts of Eastern Europe.

Chapter four appraises the strengths and weaknesses of President Carter's campaign for human rights.

Chapter five calls attention to the conflict between Stalinism and Eurocommunism. Eurocommunism could strengthen the Kremlin's hand—except for the issue of human rights in Eastern Europe.

Chapter six describes the crisis in Africa; chapter seven considers disarmament and development; chapter eight surveys South American dictatorships.

Chapter nine appraises the religious significance of the crisis, especially in Russia.

Chapter ten offers an overall view, with conclusions about the meaning of the crisis for America and the world.

The CRISIS of HUMAN RIGHTS

1
The What and Why of Human Rights

"You are walking, and any creature making a step on the dry grass behind you might be an Amin man. Whenever you hear a car speeding down the street, you think it might suddenly come to a stop—for you. I finally fled, not because I was in trouble or because of anything I did, but out of sheer fear."[1] Such is the report of an African who fled Uganda.

The 1948 United Nations Declaration of Human Rights states, "All human beings are born free and equal in dignity and rights. . . . Everyone has the right to life, liberty, and security of person. . . . No one shall be subjected to arbitrary interference with his privacy, home or correspondence, nor to attacks upon his honor and reputation. Everyone has the right to the protection of the law against such interference or attacks."[2]

It is Monday evening, October 11, 1976. Father Patrick Rice, an Irish citizen, is walking in Villa Soldata, a suburb of Buenos Aires. He is accompanied by a young Argentinian girl who has come to him for counsel. Suddenly, a man springs from an old delivery van as it approaches them and cries, "Halt or I will shoot." The stranger fires first at the ground and then into the air. He orders the priest and the girl into the van and transports them to Police Station 36.

Father Rice's shirt is put over his head. When he is asked

his name, he identifies himself as a priest and is beaten. His captors tell him the Romans treated the first Christians well in comparison to what will happen to him—he will see! With his hands tied behind his back, Father Rice is placed in the trunk of a car and the girl who accompanied him is forced to ride in the back seat. At an army casern the priest is given the water treatment: His nose is held and water is forced into his mouth. The treatment is continued most of Tuesday, with only three or four hours respite, by persons who say they belong to the Argentinian Anti-Communist Alliance.

On Wednesday, Father Rice and the girl are subjected to electric shock treatment. One guard explains, "I am against force, and for this reason we will not kill you." Father Rice is told that the reason for his apprehension is that he has been making propaganda slogans against the army. He denies the charge. He is kept in a cell Thursday and is warned to say he received his black eyes from falling downstairs; otherwise his body will be found in the river. Finally, he is washed and shaved and taken to the Irish embassy. However, he is still not released. Instead, he is imprisoned from four to five weeks after being taken to the embassy before he is deported.[3]

South American victims are not all clergymen; some are scientists. MIT physicists searched for more than a year for Dr. Antonio Misetich, who formerly taught at their university.[4] Believed to have been abducted by the police from his Buenos Aires suburban home, he was never heard of again.

Misuse of Psychiatry

Science, like religion, has worldwide outreach. Leonard Plyushch, a Russian mathematician known to his peers throughout the world, once wrote idealistically of his hope for "the creation of a truly Communist society . . . in which the spirit will be liberated from the primal needs of the stomach."[5] Acting on his idealism, he sent an open letter to the newspaper *Komsomolskaya Pravda* protesting a political trial. As a result, he was dismissed from the Cybernetics Institute of the Academy of Sciences in his native Ukraine. He had been a member of the Initiative Group for the Defense of Human Rights in Moscow since 1969 and had signed all seven of its appeals. Plyushch was arrested for anti-Soviet agitation and propaganda in January, 1972.

After his first year's imprisonment, the mathematician was examined by three psychiatric commissions. One group of specialists alleged he was suffering from reformist delusions, messianic elements, and sluggish schizophrenia. Another commission was headed by Dr. Andrei Snezhnevsky, Director of the Institute of Psychiatry of the Academy of Medical Sciences and notorious for mishandling dissidents. In an examination which lasted less than twenty minutes, Snezhnevsky asked: "How do you feel? What principles are you fighting for? Why don't you think of your family?" Subsequently, the Kiev Regional Court committed Plyushch to the special psychiatric hospital at Dnepropetrovsk, regarded by political prisoners as the most abusive. He had not been allowed to attend the court's hearing, much less to defend himself.

On arrival at Dnepropetrovsk, the "patient" was given large doses of neuroleptics in an attempt to break his will. For ten days he was quarantined with some people who were clearly mad, some who had epileptic seizures, and others who howled or writhed in pain from drugs. To sustain himself, Plyushch began reading books loaned to him by fellow inmates. Then sulphur injections and other drugs began to cloud his mind.

If an inmate refused to answer questions, the MVD (Ministry of Internal Affairs) major assigned to supervise political prisoners would say, "You see, you're not being sincere; there is a deterioration in your mental state." Notes came from other prisoners advising Plyushch to give up. A visit from his wife was allowed shortly after he had been given large doses of Haloperidol in August, 1973, without counteracting agents. Trembling and gasping for air, he could hardly speak and broke off the visit. Subsequently the mathematician was tied to a bed and given insulin. In November, 1974, he wrote to his wife saying he could no longer answer her letters. He had received large doses of Triftazin, a neuroleptic known in English as Stelazinc.

Meanwhile, Mrs. Plyushch had written to every possible source for help. One day the KGB, the secret police, stopped a bus en route from Kiev to Moscow and took her off it, interrupting her trip to ask help from friends. They threatened her with arrest and the loss of her children. Yet thanks to her activities, her husband's case became known abroad. Thousands of mathematicians from the United States and Western Europe signed petitions requesting Plyushch's release. Socialists and even Communists from France joined in the protest. The prisoner-patient was finally allowed to leave the country. With his face and body swollen from two and a half years of neuroleptic drugs, he arrived in the West in January, 1976, and was pronounced exhausted but mentally normal by the examining physician.

The world's most prestigious psychiatric body, the Sixth World Congress of Psychiatry, condemned "the systematic abuse of psychiatry for political purposes" in the USSR and all countries in which such abuses occur.[6] The resolution passed by a narrow vote in the face of Soviet opposition.

Why Human Rights?

What are the thoughts of victims who suffer from such abuse of human rights? How are their protests articulated intellectually? Dr. Jan Patocka once taught philosophy at Charles University in Prague. Seventy years old, having survived forced retirement when the Communists came to power, he was a spokesman for the Czechoslovakian Charter

77, issued at the beginning of 1977. In fact, Patocka stopped the Dutch foreign minister in a Prague hotel lobby to explain the document. A week after his arrest and a midnight interrogation by the political police, he died of a cerebral hemorrhage. Shortly before his death, Patocka wrote an open letter from Prague:

> No society, no matter how formidable its technics, can function without a moral basis, a belief that is not a matter of opportunism, circumstances, and expected benefits. But the purpose of morality is not to enable society to function; its purpose is merely to enable man to become human. . . . We therefore, believe that certain simple ideas, which have proved themselves through the shared painful experience of recent decades, should be clearly brought to the consciousness of all, and that the time for this has come.[7]

The idea of human rights pacts means "that states and societies too are subject to the sovereignty of moral sentiments—that they acknowledge something that is without qualification higher than themselves and is binding on them, inviolable and unassailable, Patocka emphasized."[8] States must also be prepared to establish and secure legal norms that serve this purpose. "No individual who truly suffers wrong should feel isolated and abandoned to the superior force of circumstances so long as he remains true to the duty of not surrendering himself," he concluded.[9]

An Issue of Principle

The basic issue can be put simply: Does not might really make right? In a large number of countries today, all opposition is labeled antisocial and a threat to the nation. If dissidents do not destroy the regime, it is argued, they will at least weaken and debilitate it. This totalitarian outlook is at the root of the contemporary crisis. The counterclaim asserts that persons are worthy of respect and have dignity and rights of their own. They are unique, not things, objects, or animals. Persons are ends in themselves rather than simply means to state goals. It is important to recognize that individual conscience and the courage to criticize can contribute to the life of the state; they do not work against it, as totalitarians fear!

One may argue that respect for human rights has often been the exception rather than the rule throughout history. Virtually from the beginning of man, tyrants have attempted to impose their will and power on their subjects. Justice is not easy to establish; yet this is no reason for cynicism. The abuse of human rights raises fundamental questions: What is the relation between good intentions and effective actions, between morality and power?

Such basic human rights as freedom of speech, press, and assembly, the liberty to choose one's own religion, freedom from hunger, and equal educational opportunity are not simple to establish. Nevertheless, difficulties in defining them in detail need not obscure their intrinsic validity and worth. It is obvious that major differences exist between rich and poor countries, new nations and older colonial powers, Communists and non-Communists, North and South, East and West. Yet there is a universal longing for justice as citizens live out their lives in hope or despair.

Classifications of Rights

Human rights are generally divided into at least three classifications. One group of rights has to do with the integrity of persons: freedom from arbitrary arrest and imprisonment, a fair public trial, and the absence of torture. Such guarantees have been recognized under a variety of governments, both monarchist and republican. Premised on the dignity of persons, these rights are considered necessary to a decent human life.

Denis Goulet, Fellow with the Overseas Development

Council, argues for the slogan "No more torture."[10] He believes it is a viable starting point for a contemporary consensus. "No credibility can be gained for a policy of promoting *all* human rights unless there is first an active and coherent commitment by governments to combat torture and mass misery energetically. . . ." This first group of rights is often defended as inherent in human nature. They cannot be taken away by the state because they have not been given by the state. Tyranny can only cripple citizens by abuse, engendering alienation and unrest.

A second group of rights more positively assures the citizen of freedom to participate in government: liberty of thought, speech, and assembly, as well as democratic elections. It also includes freedom of religion and the right to unlimited movement within and without the country.

We need to note that the American separation of church and state was an innovation. It was included in the first ten amendments of the U.S. Constitution, which were added as a bill of rights for personal liberties. Forbidding any establishment of religion by the state, these amendments guarantee the rights of freedom of speech, press, and assembly, and the right to fair trial. To be sure, critics point out that full respect for persons was not realized at once in the United States. Liberty was compromised in the unhappy legacy of slavery.

A third group of rights—food, shelter, health care, and education—have found acceptance more recently. Their defenders argue that political freedom can mean little when basic physical needs remain unsatisfied. Political guarantees are meaningless when a hungry man—tried by due process—is hanged for stealing bread. In spite of the moral decency inherent in such rights, they are often seen as ideals or goals rather than civil liberties. This classification, more than the others, raises political questions about implementation. Maurice Cranston, a British scholar, warns that the notion of rights can be expanded so far that they lose their meaning. "An ideal is something one can aim at, but cannot by definition immediately realize. A right, on the contrary, is something that can and from the moral point of view, must be respected here and now."[11]

International Sanction

Human rights have been sanctioned by a large number of international documents. Most often cited is the Universal Declaration of Human Rights, which was accepted by the United Nations in 1948. Fifteen years later, the world organization adopted two conventions, one for political rights and the other for economic rights. The more recent Helsinki treaty of 1975 has a limited geographical scope; it is a joint European-American agreement signed by thirty-five nations. But its actualization and implementation became the storm center of debate about human rights.

Historical Background

Respect for human dignity seemed to grow throughout the last century. Slavery was abolished. The world enjoyed a century of relative stability from the end of the Napoleonic era until the outbreak of World War I. Although European colonial rule was extended in Africa and Asia, wars were local rather than worldwide. The United States lived in isolation, at least until the Spanish-American War. The question of America's relation to Europe was raised afresh with the U.S. intervention in World War I, assuring an Allied victory. President Woodrow Wilson idealistically championed the League of Nations and the self-determination of peoples. But his program was rejected by both Europeans and his fellow countrymen. The United States then retreated into isolation, attempting to remain neutral even in the face of Nazism, until the attack on Pearl Harbor.

The changed ethos brought about by World War II was

symbolized by the fact that New York City became the home of the United Nations. The United States committed itself to work for justice through this organization. The wife of the wartime president, Mrs. Franklin D. Roosevelt, headed the commission that drew up the Universal Declaration of Human Rights.[12] But at the same time, millions of anti-Communist Russians who had fled to Western Europe were returned forcibly to the Soviet Union by the Allies, most of them for imprisonment and some for death. A dichotomy between ideals and practice was evident. All easy optimism about the goodness of man had been shattered. Belief in justice and dignity needed deeper roots. In such a situation, the importance of rights as negative safeguards can hardly be overstated. They are not premised on goodwill or friendship, but on the need for common decency and fair play.

Helsinki

The issue of human rights would be worldwide even without communism. However, the crisis is complicated by the power struggle between East and West, as the debate about the Helsinki accord has shown.

Secretary of State Henry Kissinger was interested in the Helsinki pact primarily as a means of gaining Russian agreement on "real issues." The USSR wanted governmental acceptance and guarantees for postwar borders. It was the Western European allies who made human rights a nonnegotiable condition of any conference. Kissinger had to reckon with a virtual ultimatum from them when he met his Russian counterpart, Andrei Gromyko, in Vienna. Gromyko is reported to have sarcastically remarked: "You don't mean to tell me that our leaders cannot get together because of disagreement over whether the Dutch are allowed to put on political cabarets in Moscow."[13] The non-Communist Europeans overcame Kissinger's reluctance and Gromyko's resistance, inserting as many human rights guarantees as possible in the final form of the Helsinki accord.

All the signatories accepted postwar borders and pledged noninterference in the domestic affairs of other nations. The Russian concern was to stabilize the situation in Europe a quarter of a century after the end of World War II. Communist and non-Communist alike signed, accepting responsibility for civil liberties. However, the agreement has produced a controversy neither Gromyko nor Kissinger anticipated.

President Carter

The election of Jimmy Carter as president of the United States marked a watershed in foreign policy with respect to human rights. Welcoming Russian dissident Vladimir Bukovsky to the White House, Carter remarked:

> Our commitment to the concept of human rights is permanent, and I don't intend to be timid in my public statements and positions. I want them to be productive and not counterproductive. And also [I want] to assure that our nation and countries other than the Soviet Union are constantly aware that we want to pursue the freedom of individuals and their right to express themselves.[14]

Carter's critics were not slow to answer. "What recent rhetoric shows," remarked Fouad Ajami, writing from Princeton's Center for International Studies, "is that the American pendulum rarely stops in the middle; it swings from one extreme to another."[15] He described contemporary "moralism and sermons" as in part therapy and catharsis. In today's discourse, he warned, lie the "seeds of future disillusionment with human rights." After a year or two of posturing, he predicted, Americans will conclude that the venture has failed and they had better return to a more "realistic" foreign policy.

Survey of Abuse

When President Ford was still in office, congressmen asked Secretary of State Kissinger for information on the abuse of human rights in countries receiving U.S. aid.[16] Kissinger replied that any overall survey was impractical. Nevertheless, Congress enacted legislation requiring periodic reports by law.

A 143-page document was published shortly after the beginning of President Carter's term in office. Thirteen fundamental rights recognized by the United Nations had been investigated by U.S. diplomats in the eighty-two nations that receive U.S. funds. The list included protection from personal violence, the right to a fair trial, due process of law, and freedoms of expression: religion, assembly, travel, and association. The investigation showed that the press works under the threat of government restriction in fifty-two of the countries. Police torture has taken place in at least thirty-two of the eighty-two states. Blanket security laws allowing governments to suspend civil liberties and to hold persons in imprisonment without trial are widespread. Only twenty-three of eighty-two nations had acceptable records.

In the wake of disillusionment about Vietnam, the popular attitude often has been, you can't change things, so why try?[17] Praise or blame for conduct is withheld; there is only the familiar litany of disillusionment. Persons of this conviction cite the bewildering effect of American culture on others that cannot handle it or do not want it, the failure of expensive programs to alleviate problems, and the discovery that playing the world's "nanny" as well as the world's policeman endears you to no one.

Critics point out that a value-free attitude appeals to persons who are nervous about human rights and has been advocated as a form of no-nonsense professionalism by diplomatic technocrats. Public discussion of a dictator's misdeeds may ruin a deal with his country. Complaint about violation of human rights came to be viewed as almost subversive during the Nixon years. Diplomats who took this line were not necessarily "pink," but they were considered to be "yellow," lacking the courage for high office. It was as if the United States was to be defended against the rest of the world, make profits from it, and otherwise remain as undisturbed as possible. More often than not, such practicality and selfishness bred a narrow and sterile foreign policy. Insofar as the United States had any human rights diplomacy, it came from Congress and was opposed by the president.

Congressional interest has made human rights diplomacy not simply a question of U.N. debate, but of American foreign policy. U.S. power, although not unlimited, is probably greater than that of any other nation in the world, rivaled only by Russia. But in many countries the U.S. has no leverage to help victims of oppression. Americans can deplore atrocities in places like Cambodia, but little can be done about them. The United States does, however, have influence in nations that depend heavily on it for their economic and military survival. It can give or withhold diplomatic support, trade advantages, credits, arms, and money. Human rights diplomacy can be decisive. Although U.S. options are more limited with respect to the Soviet Union and its Eastern European satellites, even there U.S. acquiescence or opposition to the abuse of civil liberties is important.

Everyone knows that human rights violations are not words in a debate. Mere rhetoric will not correct them. Responsible and realistic policies are called for. Unfortunately, it is cheaper for rulers to terrorize populations than to meet popular substantive and legal demands. Various parts of the world have different problems, opportunities, and limitations.

Growing Crisis

Hope was expressed that newly established countries, liberated from colonial rule, would respect human rights. In reality, this dream has often failed. Dictatorial regimes have multiplied even more rapidly than expected.

In Togo, West Africa, on January 13, 1963, soldiers who had recently been demobilized from the French colonial army revolted.[18] The military coup which brought a change of government was condemned by the Organization of African Unity. Soon, however, it gave up such protest. During the next five years, sixty-four uprisings took place in African countries. In South America, popular democracy suffered major setbacks as dictatorships took over in Brazil (1964) and in Chile (1973). The crisis is more ominous because Stalinism has now reappeared in force in the USSR. Party Secretary Khrushchev denounced the excesses of Stalin from the Kremlin itself in 1956. A decade later, political trials of dissidents had begun again. Stalinism was the ideological basis of the repression of the Prague Spring in 1968.

The defense of human rights need not imply that the United States can remold the rest of the world in its own image. Cultural traditions are diverse. Efforts to impose parliamentary democracy, for example, have often led to caricatures. On the other hand, the absence of free elections has bred tyranny. Goulet urges that policy "should not take the form of a crusading spirit which flaunts U.S. superiority on rights, but should rather rise from a sense of our own interests and security [as they] are increasingly dependent on the protection of human dignity throughout the world."[19] Respect for the dignity of persons is primary, and political organization is a necessary tool toward this end. A human rights policy needs to favor governments that are responsive to their own citizens, even when they do not conform fully to the American model. It should be characterized by coherence, a single standard, and activism.

In a careful survey, Goulet argues that the term "human rights" can be expressed effectively in policy only if it is not used too broadly or too narrowly.[20] It is used too broadly for policy purposes when it includes all the ideas embraced in the U.N. Declaration of Human Rights. Even when the idea is defined with relative precision, it touches so many areas of policy as to risk diffuseness and utopian wishfulness. Applicable ground rules cannot be developed from intellectual reflection alone; policy experimentation in a variety of settings is necessary. All the rights sanctioned in the U.N. documents are, of course, significant. Yet taken together they are so comprehensive as to exclude effective monitoring. On the other hand, the list of rights ought not to be reduced to a bare minimum.

Justice is never complete amid conflicting claims in different situations. Yet this consideration need not lead to the abandonment in principle of belief in the worth and dignity of persons or to the affirmation that right and wrong are simply arbitrary. The contemporary crisis is compounded by the fact that modern technology multiplies new tools of oppression. Dictatorships attempt to impose uniformity through thought control, insisting on their own absoluteness. A sound policy should make clear that human rights cannot be given away for political convenience or expediency. In principle, human rights are nonnegotiable.

French philosopher Jacques Maritain, writing on *Man and the State*, observed that individuals coming from the four corners of the earth and belonging "not only to different cultures and civilizations, but to different spiritual families and antagonistic schools of thought" can find agreement in concern for human rights.[21] They can agree on practical objectives. Describing one of the meetings of the French National Commission of the United Nations, Maritain recalled how the topic was being discussed. "Someone was astonished that certain proponents of violently opposed ideologies concurred on a draft list of rights—provided no one asked why." But the question of "why" cannot be avoided. Religious faith commitments—what men really believe—become apparent in the face of tyranny.

2
Why There are Dissidents in Russia

The USSR denies its citizens free contact with the outside world. At the end of World War II, Stalin imprisoned hundreds of thousands, probably millions, of persons who had come to know Western Europeans or Americans. Today, travel and residence in Russia continue to be controlled by a system of internal passports; the public is not allowed free movement from place to place. Critics of the regime cannot publish or speak openly. Newspapers, radio, and television dispense government propaganda. All of life is organized by the party. The state is the sole employer. A citizen cannot even pray or worship God except at state-registered churches.

Russian dissidents are not revolutionaries. Their protest has been an open one in defense of human rights. In a system where police control is direct and constant, dissidents refuse to conform. When others submit, they protest. In a land with a rich cultural heritage that includes religion, they affirm the past, not just the present. Against atheism, many accept belief in God.

The ideas and activities of dissidents are known in the West because the Soviet Union is not a completely closed society. The regime wishes trade and scientific exchange with the West. Western correspondents stationed in Moscow gather information about human rights violations from protesters. But dissidents are not a Western product; they have come to the West with their charges, looking for encouragement. To be sure, without foreign contacts their protests would take a very different form.

It is important not to overstate the number and influence of Russian dissidents. Although the Russian press, radio, and television have made them widely known by campaigns against them, they have no major following among the masses. The possibility of their influence among intellectuals is a greater one. The Kremlin's sensitivity to outside protest on behalf of human rights approaches paranoia.

The West can protect few, if any, dissidents from harassment or imprisonment, although foreign contacts have kept some persons alive and led to the release and exile of others. The USSR's long campaign of repression began with the 1967 prosecution and conviction of two writers who had sent materials critical of the regime to the West—Yuli Daniel and Andrei Sinyavsky. The attack against the dissidents in the name of patriotism has grown with détente. Unfortunately, it has not brought a relaxation of repression in Russia. Early in the development of détente, Makhail Suslov warned that the era of peaceful coexistence would see no letup in the struggle between capitalism and communism "in the spheres of ideology, politics, and economics."[1]

Solzhenitsyn

Members of the ruling elite—party functionaries, literary figures, high government officials—had assembled in a large hall on the outskirts of Moscow while Nikita Khrushchev was still in power.[2] Suddenly the Party Secretary interrupted their conversation and raised his hands in applause. "Comrades," he exclaimed, "Solzhenitsyn is among us." A tall, awkward-looking man whose suit fitted badly and who seemed out of place, Solzhenitsyn received the adulation modestly. In reality, he had already turned from Marxism to Christianity even while Khrushchev was reactivating the antireligious campaign.

Khrushchev had personally authorized publication of Solzhenitsyn's novel about the work camps as part of his anti-Stalinist campaign. Solzhenitsyn's exposure was without parallel. In careful detail and without emotion, he narrated the Stalinist terror which had reached into a large part of Russian households. Solzhenitsyn's other books were never published officially in Russia. Following Khrushchev's fall from power, the dissident was expelled from the Writers' Union. Endlessly harassed by the secret police at the same time he received the Nobel Prize for literature, he was finally forced into exile. Today his works circulate in underground *samizdat* (self-published) copies, made in part from the broadcasts of Radio Liberty.

Solzhenitsyn was one of millions of political prisoners released from Stalin's Gulag Archipelago while Khrushchev was in power. Khrushchev's criticism of the dictator at the Twentieth Party Congress in 1956 marked the high point of reform. When Khrushchev was displaced by the old bureaucracy, dissidents like Solzhenitsyn recognized a return to Stalinism.

The Crisis

The crisis of human rights in Eastern European Communist countries is a permanent one.[3] Unrest seems to be built into the very structure of the society. It flares up at some moments and dies down at others, primarily because governments do not wish to return to the open terror of the Stalin period. Official policy oscillates between bouts of repression and intervals of partial tolerance. It seeks some midpoint of stability, but this is not to be found. Every short-term "solution" brings new difficulties. The Communist party bureaucracy, attempting to control all of life and culture, again and again develops an atmosphere incompatible with even minimal human freedom.

Moral-religious resistance has practical political implications in Eastern Europe, as Communist functionaries know only too well. The tendency to move from political demands to moral absolutes shows itself again and again as attempts to effect change are frustrated. The personal need to find life's meaning in something greater than oneself continues to have unsettling consequences.

If the ruling elite is to retain a monopoly of power, it cannot allow opposing voices to reach the masses of the people. Even though most known opponents of the regime have been arrested, new voices appear. In a situation in which there is no official opposition, unofficial opposition seems almost inevitable.

What the Dissidents Do

Dissidents have collected and disseminated information, notably the *Chronicle of Human Rights in the USSR*. In contrast with the official press, the *Chronicle* is objectively written without emotion or propaganda; feelings about arrest have been suppressed. Dissidents have formed organizations such as the Committee to Monitor the Observance of the 1975 Helsinki Pact. They attend court proceedings and have demonstrated in such places as Red Square. The answer of the secret police has been drastic: violence, banishment to work camps, and expulsion from the country. Scientists as well as nationalist leaders from the Ukraine, the Baltic states, and the Crimea have been arrested. Tartars have been taken into custody along with Jews, Buddhists, Baptists, and Orthodox Christians.

Irina Orlov, a diminutive, vivacious woman, has traveled to Lefortovo Prison once a month with a food parcel for her husband.[4] Her gift packages are restricted to two pounds each of sausage and biscuits, a pound each of sugar and cheese, and a little more than four pounds of fruits and vegetables. She is never permitted to see her husband. The stocky, red-haired physicist is charged with slandering the Soviet system. His real offense was monitoring the human rights obligations the Kremlin assumed in signing the Helsinki accord.

The Helsinki monitoring group, observes Christopher Wren, chief of the Moscow Bureau of the New York *Times*, was a victim of too much success.[5] The physicist's two-room apartment in southwest Moscow had become a clearinghouse for reports of human rights violations. These were compiled and channeled to the West. Similar monitoring groups had sprung up in the Ukraine, Lithuania, Georgia, and Armenia. Together, they struck a response from more than the small body of dissidents who usually support human rights campaigns. Jewish leaders formed a link with the activistic communities. Blue-collar Baptists, Pentecostals, and Seventh-day Adventists contributed accounts of religious persecution. The Orlov group even noted governmental interference in postal services and travel abroad. Police raided apartments in Moscow and Kiev, closed down the monitoring groups, and confiscated their files.

Religious Persecution

On June 17, 1976, before Orlov's arrest, the Moscow group released its fifth published document.[6] It called attention to the persecution of families of religious believers. Citing specific laws, it reported that USSR ideological policy seeks control of the total formation of children through Communist education. A child can be taken from his parents and parental rights denied if he is being brought up under "antisocial influence."

The report showed that courts have moved in particular against Baptists, Pentecostals, and Seventh-day Adventists.

Eleven cases were cited involving numerous persons: M. Suprunovitch, a Baptist, lost the right to educate her three children; they were turned over to their atheist father. Attempts have been made to take away the older daughter of an Adventist mother, Marija Vlasjuc. Schoolteachers have threatened children of religious parents with court action. A school director in Frunze told an Adventist child, Irina Luzenko, "I have already killed two of your sort and I will send you to a special school, the work colony for youth." Heavy fines, many of which cannot be paid, have been assessed. Houses where believers have assembled for prayer have been destroyed. The committee concludes that all this is in crass contradiction to the Helsinki accord.

Dismissed by the official press as "a tiny group of nonentities who represent no one and nothing," the Helsinki monitors posed a threat that could not be ignored. The police clamped down. But for everyone arrested there is someone waiting to take his place.

Anti-Semitism

The role of anti-Semitism in the campaign against the dissidents tells much about the situation. Following the revolution, the Communists under Lenin honored the cultural autonomy of a variety of nationalities. A large number of Jewish persons, most with negligible religious ties, participated in the Communist movement. Stalin crushed the idealism of the revolution, executing Lenin's comrades. Through his encouragement, anti-Semitism began to spread throughout Russian society. It has been the regime's intention that Jewishness should be at most a nationality and not a religion, but religion does not die so easily.

The phenomenon is now an oft-repeated one. Persons of Jewish heritage who had given up religious practice and even belief in God begin to recover their heritage. Refusing to assimilate, they reassert Jewish identity, traditional loyalty, and faith. After the Six-Day War of 1967, Israel had additional dramatic appeal for such persons, especially in the face of totalitarian oppression and renewed anti-Semitism.

Jewish Protest

"I request for the second time that you return to me the materials required for the observance of the historical traditions connected with this festival; the Bible and the Hagadah."[7] So Lazar Lyubarsky wrote to the Rostov public procurator, protesting that these things had been illegally confiscated from his apartment. He described the refusal of the procurator to return the articles as "a deliberate act which completely destroyed our family observance of Passover, . . . profoundly offended my national dignity, . . . a profanation of the ancient and holy festival." Lyubarsky and his daughter also wrote to President Podgorny.

In time, some of the materials were returned and the criminal case against him was discontinued. But he persisted in claiming his rights, and new charges were made against him. In consequence, he received a four-year jail sentence. Fellow religionists in Vilna, Moscow, Leningrad, and Kharkov went on a hunger strike during his trial.

Leonard Schroeter, author of *The Last Exodus*, observes that Lyubarsky deliberately courted disaster.[8] A "principled Jew, made of the stuff of the Old Testament prophets," he showed the dogged, daring behavior that also characterizes Solzhenitsyn and Vladimir Bukovsky. Why? After years of guarded conversations, surreptitious reading, and the sharing of nonpermitted thoughts with one's closest friends, some intellectuals finally revolt. Schroeter finds that the regime replies with a kind of madness. Many of those in authority are cynical, some anti-Semitic.

Soviet judges, prosecutors, or KGB men see opposition as

treason and regard a natural interest, identification, and desire for contact with one's national brethren or coreligionists as illicit, subversive conspiracy.[9]

Russian Jewish dissidents seeking to leave for Israel make up one party; other dissidents expect or wish to remain in Russia.

Foreign Affairs Protest

On August 25, 1968, four days after the Soviet invasion of Czechoslovakia, seven citizens demonstrated against their government's crushing of dissent in another land.[10] Standing on Red Square, they unfurled their banners—"Hands Off Czechoslovakia"; "For Your Freedom and Ours." Plainclothesmen dragged the group into police cars. One was a thirty-two-year-old woman holding a three-month-old child in her arms. Natalia Gorbanevskaya, a poet, was a member of the Moscow Human Rights Movement. Since she was the sole support of her family, she was released, but after Mrs. Gorbanevskaya reported the demonstration in the underground *samizdat* press, she was taken into custody again.

At the Serbsky Institute she was diagnosed as insane. A court review (that neither she nor members of her family were allowed to attend) confirmed the judgment: "Extensive psychopathy, not excluding the possible presence of a sluggish schizophrenic process" requiring "compulsory treatment in a psychiatric hospital of a special type." Mrs. Gorbanevskaya was among fifteen political prisoners in the women's ward of a special psychiatric hospital at Kazan. Kept separated from each other, they could meet only during exercise periods or in the toilets. Half the group had been confined for their religious beliefs.

Mrs. Gorbanevskaya reports that her first reaction was one of "insurmountable horror." She did not know how long she would be at the hospital or in what state she would end up. It was almost impossible for her to concentrate on anything because the doctors gave her Haloperidol. This drug, marketed in the United States as Haldol, is a potent neuroleptic. As such, it causes extreme "psychomotor excitation." The patient cannot be still for any period of time—sitting, lying, or standing. The drug makes sleep impossible. A counteracting drug was in short supply. Finally, Mrs. Gorbanevskaya conceded that she probably should not have engaged in dissident activities and "even this morsel satisfied them." In December, 1975, she was allowed to emigrate with her two children.

Amnesty International

Other forms of intimidation were used. A Soviet Amnesty International member, Mykola Rudenko, appealed for help for a Kiev physician, Mychajlo Spyrydonovyc Kovtunenko.[11] Rudenko reported that the doctor had never read *samizdat* underground documents. Day and night he had labored, even in rain and snow, caring for people. Now the physician was in prison while his wife, daughter, and mother remained at home. "I appeal to all men in the wide world; raise **your** voice to defend the physician, M. S. Kovtunenko. He is a knight of the spirit and science. He is a true humanist. He remained true to his Hippocratic Oath. He is a true son of his suffering Ukranian homeland."

On April 18, 1975, Rudenko was arrested for his activities for Amnesty International, but was detained only two days. Because he was a war invalid, officials did not want to keep him in prison on the thirtieth anniversary celebration of the Russian victory over the Germans. Before his own arrest, the physician wrote with a shaking hand, "I, M. S. Kovtunenko, was asked by the KGB to observe and spy on Mykola Rudenko, as he is against the government and belongs to the Sakharov Group. I share fully and completely the opinions of Mykola Rudenko and will defend him as much as possible. I am of the opinion that we have no freedom, not even the most elementary. I believe in the Ukraine."

Vladimir Bukovsky

It is Russian dissident Vladimir Bukovsky, more than anyone, who has exposed the Soviet misuse of psychiatry. In particular, he has protested the use of drug injections at mental hospitals in the suppression of dissidents, although Bukovsky himself does not seem to have been given such treatment. The Christian concern of Hans Kristian, a member of the International Sakharov Hearing, led to Bukovsky's release in exchange for Chilean Communist party leader Luis Corvalan. Kristian went first to the Russian embassy in Switzerland and later negotiated with Chilean officials. Following his release, Bukovsky addressed the Free German Association in Berlin. "The frontiers of freedom are not just on one side or the other of the Berlin Wall," he said. "In reality, the frontiers of freedom and lack of freedom are much more complicated. They lie inside each one of us."

> True, over there we are in a prison. But a man can retain freedom of choice, can he not, even in prison? He can leave prison if he pays the price of betrayal. . . . He can demean himself to obtain some small favor, or he can fight. . . .

Bukovsky reports that there is this much freedom in prison. Moreover, a man who is not free within himself easily finds a mass of self-justifying arguments.

> The temptations of his captive state are created, he may tell himself, by noble aims which can calm even the conscience of a hangman: "If I do not, someone else will. . . ." How often I have heard this argument from wardens, interrogators and prison psychiatrists.[12]

At the height of the Stalin terror, Bukovsky observes, incarceration in psychiatric prison hospitals was a humane strategy. More recently, however, under the direction of the KGB, the situation has changed. The Snerhnevsky school, with headquarters at the Serbsky Institute in Moscow, freely diagnoses prisoners as mentally ill; it supports their confinement and medication at mental hospitals under the rubric of sluggish schizophrenia. Bukovsky himself was arrested because he made two photocopies of Yugoslavian Milovan Djilas' book *The New Class*. His interrogator attempted to make him repent and give information about persons who had helped him. When this did not succeed, Bukovsky was declared mentally ill and sent to Leningrad. He was released in February, 1965. He believes his freedom resulted from the dispute between the Leningrad and Moscow schools. Professor Sluchevsky and the Leningrad school do not concur with Dr. Snerhnevsky.

Bukovsky was rearrested at the end of 1965 when he led a human rights demonstration in defense of Yuri Daniel and Andrei Sinyavsky under the slogan "Respect Your Constitution." His courage was evident by the fact that the last such demonstration had been in 1927. Bukovsky was sent to a hospital in Moscow for punishment, but its doctors did not find him insane. Then he was transferred to the Serbsky Institute, where he was confined for six months. When his mother protested to General Svetlichny, head of the KGB in Moscow, the general stomped his feet and screamed, "He will never be released. We will let him rot in the insane asylum!" In the end, it was international contacts that were effective. A representative of Amnesty International told the Director of the Institute that the case would be raised before the Bertrand Russell Tribunal if Bukovsky was not released at once.

While in the hospital, Bukovsky learned the well-established routine of psychiatric repression that had become common by the end of the 1960s. Persons most likely to receive drug treatment include religious believers, persons whose trial would bring undesirable publicity and criticism in the West, and so-called revisionist Marxists. Indeed, anyone who stands up for his legal rights is a potential victim. Bukovsky estimates that political prisoners are being treated for mental illness in at least eleven hospitals. Doctors, both male and female, are under the direction of the Ministry of Internal Affairs as MVD officers. Orderlies are often petty criminals. Even the labor camps, described in Solzhenitzyn's *One Day in the Life of Ivan Denisovich*, were more tolerable.

Bukovsky believes that the Communist ideology "has been so discredited in the Soviet Union that you would be hard put to it to find anybody who would want to build a new world on that basis." He is emphatic: "I would like to say, once and for all, that . . . communism, as a means of oppression of the people, is in no way different from fascism." The dissident emphasizes that "everybody in the Soviet Union lives a double life." In public, they speak the Marxist language forced upon them by the authorities. In private, they "use a human language which has nothing of the Marxist vocabulary." Marxist ideology remains as a shell. "The only thing the state stands on is the obedience of the people—on their submissiveness, their belief that they cannot change things."

Learned Helplessness

Bukovsky tells of an episode when he was on a Siberian expedition.[13] Three ants fell into his aluminum mug. Of course they tried to get out. He kept shaking them back into the bottom of the mug. They made a hundred, perhaps a hundred seventy attempts. And each time he shook them back into the mug. "And then, suddenly, they stopped trying. They remained at the bottom of that mug, and I left them on the grass, and there they stayed for one day, two days. . . ." Bukovsky believes that the same thing has happened to people in the Soviet Union. The psychological term for it is "learned helplessness." "A person or animal no longer believes in the possibility of rescue or change." For this reason, "the dissident movement has great meaning not only for those who remain in Russia, but for those who live abroad as well. It is the awareness of a personal, individual responsibility."

An Analysis

Andrei Amalrik, before his exile, had already become known for his writings in the West. He believes that if the regime persists in its stubbornness and allows the abuse of human rights to reach catastrophic proportions, the results will be appalling.[14] A great fund of accumulated hatred exists among the Soviet people, he reports. It is a product of all the irrationality and frustration of Soviet life. There are no channels for venting these frustrations as there are in Western democratic countries. Amalrik notes an increased role of scientists in protests, for they are accustomed to think for themselves more than others are. Like workers and peasants, they listen to foreign radio broadcasts. A morning's coffee may begin with a discussion of the latest BBC news.

Amalrik believes the people of his country have undergone an extraordinary process of education over the past few years. Slowly, some of them are beginning to think for themselves. The dissident movement is largely responsible. Campaigns against its leaders have brought it into public view and although it is small, the movement is a barometer.

Amalrik emphasizes the contrast between pre-revolutionary political movements and the modern dissidents. Before the 1917 Communist revolution, it was widely believed that man would change only after the society in which he lives is fundamentally transformed. The current dissident movement holds the reverse: First one must develop a sense of moral responsibility, transforming the minds of men. Amalrik does not think a mass movement is necessary for effective change. The life of the average citizen in the USSR is a string of endless indignities, he asserts. The bureaucracy is overbearing and arbitrary. Dissidents help ordinary people understand the nature of the system that perpetuates indignities; they challenge its totalitarian character.

Popular democracy has never been allowed to take root in the USSR. Tsarist Russia reacted defensively against the Reformation. Renaissance and Enlightenment influence came only through absolute monarchs like Peter the Great. Tolerance and freedom of conscience were denied by the tsars until the twentieth century. Now, modern dissidents challenge totalitarianism in the name of freedom, many of them on religious grounds. When men are not free to worship God and choose their own life values, human existence becomes tragically one-dimensional.

A Satire

Alexander Zinoviev, professor of logic at the Moscow Institute of Philosophy, was dismissed from his position after his novel *Yawning Heights* reached the West.[15] Its 561 pages are a witty and abstruse commentary on the human condition and life in the USSR. The author mocks and ridicules, jokes and frolics, weeps and whines in every key. He includes comments on religion more as an inquirer than a defender.

The novel is set in the imaginary land of Ibansk. "Be careful," one of Zinoviev's characters warns a foreign journalist who always seems to turn up whenever some intelligent piece of stupidity is about to be proclaimed. "You are on a visit to the society of the future." Ibansk is the home of Socism, a doctrine that has been worked out to its logical conclusion. The reference to Stalinism is clear in the description of an age of bankruptcy when part of the population was confined in camps while another part guarded them and the remainder saw to it that nothing ever changed. This is past, however. How does one get to Ibansk now?

The citizen must make formal application, filling out a questionnaire to show that neither he nor his relatives have ever considered taking a trip abroad, much less failed to observe the duty of Silence. When all this has been done, one need not ask where Ibansk is; he is there already. Its society is the most perfect, the most humane, and the most free. If one comes across anything bad in the world, he must remember it does not exist in Ibansk because, in principle, nothing bad can exist there. A mistake cannot exist in Ibansk since, a priori, it is not possible in an ideal place.

A dualism divides Zinoviev's characters. On one side are establishment academics, scientists, artists, writers, journalists, and party bureaucrats. On the other side is the opposition, which is able to think but not act. The opposition is given names by the bureaucracy: the Talker, the Slanderer, the Pharisee, the Schizophrenic. The Seeker after Truth is probably Solzhenitsyn. Non-thinking establishment names sound like orders and decorations: Thinker, Sociologist, Teacher, Theorist, Scientist, Secretary, Pretender, and Collaborator. The official cliché-ridden language stands in contrast to the uncensored language of the opposition.

The Careerist makes fun of the proposal of the Seeker After Truth that official ideology should be abandoned on the ground that no one takes it seriously. The Talker takes issue:

The origin and development of an ideology is outside human control. It is an impenetrable secret, and will remain one, though it takes place before our eyes. So long as men are in a position to influence ideology, they do not know what ideology is. And if they begin to guess, it's too late. . . . The attitude to the official ideology is the most important element in the system of selection—on the road to power.[16]

Ibansk conquers the world; all opposition is wiped out.

One day a new law is promulgated in Ibansk. Citizens will be permitted to commit suicide upon reaching a pensionable age. There is no coercion in the matter, but everyone applies.

3

The Survival of Freedom in the Satellites

In late summer of 1968, Russian tanks rolled into Prague. The repression of human rights in Eastern Europe was illustrated most dramatically by this military occupation. The crisis continues as the majority of the Czechoslovakian population has not become reconciled to the regime. Charter 77 was released in Prague at the beginning of 1977 and before the year's end, leading signers had been sentenced to jail terms of up to three years in intensified repression.

Human rights have suffered in Czechoslovakia ever since its betrayal to Hitler at Munich. The country is in a region which has for centuries been a center of struggle between the great powers. When it was given political independence after World War I, Czechoslovakia established a popularly based democracy. The "Father of the Country," Thomas Masaryk, was inspired by Protestant Christian concepts of freedom. In 1948, the Communists took over, apparently murdering Masaryk's son. They seemed in firm control of the country, allied with Russia, until the Prague Spring of 1968.

Charter 77

Charter 77 appeals for the observance of the Helsinki accord. The freedom and rights of man as guaranteed by this document, it protests, exist only on paper in Czechoslovakia.[1] Tens of thousands of citizens are denied work in their respective fields of specialization because they do not agree with official views. A host of young people are refused higher education by reason of their parents' political past. Victims of many-sided discrimination are robbed of virtually every opportunity, their lives sacrificed to a kind of apartheid. At the same time, hundreds of thousands of citizens live under the threat of losing their positions and other opportunities if they express their real opinions. Not only are human rights denied, but even a minor deviation from established ideology—political, philosophical, scientific, or artistic—brings reprisals.

On January 6, 1977, the secret police arrested three men who had been delegated to deliver the Charter to the government—before they reached their destination. This action illustrates the way private life is interfered with as the Charter asserts. The Communist bureaucracy has become both judge and sole administrative power. Citizens confined to jail are in danger of losing their health; others are not allowed to leave the country. Charter 77 also protests that there is no freedom of religion. Religious instruction is discouraged by the state, and the clergy fear loss of necessary government permission to exercise their office.

More than seven hundred persons took the risk of signing Charter 77. Among them was the Czech war hero and lifelong Communist General Vilem Sacher. He explained his reasons for taking part in the protest: "I believed in communism with human rights. Where do you think that exists? It doesn't exist anywhere in the world, but in 1968 we were ready to go for socialism with human rights. The government here does not respect human rights. Charter 77 is the difference between real life and state documents—a dual between the truth and a lie."[2] Workers at the huge CKD factory in Prague believed similarly. Only twenty-two of seven thousand appeared at a rally to denounce the Charter. *Rude Pravo*, the Communist party newspaper, attempted to bury the Charter in threats and contempt.

> The Charter was produced at the order of anti-Communist and Zionist centres in the West. They know well in these cold war staff rooms that people can no longer be duped by fairy tales about Bolsheviks eating babies. And so they hire waverers, political corpses, spineless people ready to lend their names to the devil, and disoriented individuals who are up to their ears in the service of the blackest imperial reaction.[3]

A January 12 editorial dubbed the "so-called Charter 77" as "an anti-state, anti-socialist rag" and added that "those who lie on the rails to stop the train of history must expect to have their legs chopped off."[4]

Reasons

Was the protest worth it all? One of the Charter's three designated spokesmen was Dr. Jan Patocka, who taught philosophy at Charles University in Prague until the Communist putsch of 1948. A translator of Hegel into the Czech language, he also wrote on Aristotle, Edmund Husserl, and Comenius. After his death the police broke up a small seminar of academicians who had assembled to discuss his philosophical works. In his last will, Patocka wrote:

> In the past, no conformity has yet led to any improvement in the situation, only a worsening. The greater the fear and servility the more brazen have the authorities become. . . . It is possible that repression may be intensified. . . . People can lose even those jobs which until now seemed a safe haven—night watchmen, window cleaners, stockers, hospital orderlies, etc.,

[but] not for long, since these jobs have to be done by somebody.[5]

He concluded, "People are again aware that there are things for which it is worthwhile to suffer. . . . [They are the things] which make life worth living."[6]

Cecil Parrott, formerly a British ambassador to Czechoslovakia, reports that since Charter 77 police surveillance has been stepped up to the point of intolerable harassment.[7] Most remaining leaders of the Prague Spring were given menial jobs, and many literally flee physical contact with foreigners in fear of reprisals. Parrott concludes that the campaign against Charter 77 has taken on a paranoid dimension. There has been merciless persecution of suspected opposition leaders in the press and television. Citizens speak of a mini *heydrichiada*, a term they applied to the savage terror of the Hitler occupation, and of a "ghetto," but this time not for Jews. Persecution is directed against certain "undesirable citizens," their relatives, friends, and visitors. To keep their positions, some persons have been forced to sign a counterproposal to Charter 77 even when officials have not allowed them to read the Charter "because not even the people at the very top have seen it."

The Center for the Study of Religion and Communism at Keston College in Kent, England, reports the arrest of more than a hundred Roman Catholic priests since the signing of the Helsinki agreement,[8] although *The Christian Science Monitor* says this figure may be too high.[9] Some clergy may only have been dismissed from their parishes. Hundreds of churches are reported to be without clergy.

Only seven Protestant clergymen were among the signers of Charter 77, and they have maintained close ties with each other. They are followers of the late Professor J. L. Hromadka, founder of the Christian Peace Conference. Reprisals against Protestant leaders include not only arrest, but also job and educational penalties on their families and, of course, publication restrictions.

Evaluation

The dangerous situation in Eastern Europe does not have its origin in West European and American concern for human rights; it only confirms it. For more than two decades it has been evident that short of war, outside help for Eastern Europe is limited. The first revolt occurred in East Berlin in 1953 when workers fought tanks with stones. Revolts in Hungary in 1956 and in Czechoslovakia in 1968 were paralleled by internal unrest in Poland. The Russians have attempted to stabilize the situation through the Helsinki accord, demanding the recognition of existing borders. The Sonnefield doctrine, enunciated by a subordinate of Kissinger, consigned Eastern Europe to Russian domination in order that a concern for human rights would not lead to war between the great powers. But the hunger for freedom and personal dignity remains.

Eastern European Communist regimes would find it very dangerous to conform fully to the Helsinki human rights provisions. In fact, full freedom of information, assembly, and religion could drastically alter, and indeed destroy, the status quo. Marxist ideology and practice have not been convincing to the majority of the population.

Governments in the so-called satellite countries of Eastern Europe did not come to power by free and open elections. Except for Czechoslovakia, their bureaucracies were installed by the Russian army following World War II. Everywhere in Eastern Europe, state power is held by Communist party functionaries. The old ruling classes were destroyed, religion was persecuted, and civil rights were abrogated. The dictatorship of the proletariat meant that private property was abolished and large farms were collectivized. (This is not fully the case in Poland.) Occupation strategy varied from place to place. A diversity of cultural traditions and economic levels had to be dealt with because some countries were more industrially developed than others. In general, however, Stalinism was dominant. It met resistance, subsequently, from major forces—nationalism and the demand for human rights.

Czechoslovakia

Even before World War I, the area that is now Czechoslovakia had major industrial development. Prague, the Czechoslovakian capital, still has all the splendor of its Counter-Reformation past. Neither the land nor its people were destroyed, except for the Jews, during the Nazi occupation. Before 1968, a visitor could not have guessed easily what attitudes lay beneath the surface. As in the Austro-Hungarian empire, the people had shown strong elements of submission. Prior to the Prague Spring, Czechoslovakia was Russia's most complacent and trusted ally. But Czechoslovakian history also has had remarkable moments of self-assertion.

Judged in historical perspective, the Prague Spring was a turning point comparable only with the Russian-Chinese break. It is well known that Soviet military intervention took place only after some hesitation. A highly sophisticated movement, marked by idealism as well as remarkable working-class and intellectual participation, was put down ruthlessly. The Prague Spring, much more than Khrushchev's anti-Stalinist speech, was the shock that forced West European Communists to begin to dissent from the Kremlin's authority.

The historical significance of events in Czechoslovakia cannot yet be fully appraised. "Normalization" involves continuing sanctions against a large part of the population. Russian secret police became involved in repression even at the local level. Artistic creativity has disappeared. Widespread despair and cynicism are evident. Communist ideology is believed by only a very few. Interior Minister Jaromir Obzina identified the first target in the campaign against Charter 77 as the 40,000 persons who had refused to vote in the last election.[10] If they were not scared off from signing the Charter, he warned, as many as two million others might sign it.

Hungary

Both Hungary and Czechoslovakia belonged to the old Austro-Hungarian Hapsburg empire. The contrast between the Hungarian and Czechoslovakian situations deserves attention. Hungary is much less restless. French political scientist Raymond Aron concludes that the 1956 Hungarian Revolution, unlike the Prague Spring, really succeeded.[11] It brought a lessening of repression under so-called Gulash communism, which emphasizes a better standard of living rather than ideology. Since order was restored, the Kadar regime has been a moderate one, granting a variety of smaller privileges and freedoms. A Hungarian group openly endorsed Charter 77.

The Kadar regime has not insisted on party membership for all those holding major positions. Hungarian publications endorse international movements for human rights, as they did the Helsinki accord.[12] Citizens with good police records can travel to the West every two or three years. The country has been modernized and industrialized. Foreign contacts made possible by the reduction of international tensions contribute toward this end. In sum, the average Hungarian has learned how far he can go. Party discipline is still in force. There are unspoken rules. Also important is the fact that the Hungarians make up a unique, self-contained linguistic group; alone with the Finns, they speak a Ural-Altaic language in Europe.

Poland

An uprising in Poland in 1970 brought about the downfall of Party Secretary Wladyslaw Gomulka. Marxism has no categories for such proletarian revolt against it, and the party leader could not understand why the port cities of Danzig and Stettin were in flames.[13] His successor, Edward Gierek, has not avoided similar unrest. On June 25, 1976, workers in Radom set fire to the Communist party house and others tore up railroad tracks in Ursus on the line that links Poland with the West. They protested a government announcement of a food price rise of as much as one hundred percent. Many workers spend up to half their incomes for food alone.

Almost immediately after police intervention and arrests, a committee for the defense of the workers was organized. It raised two and a half million zlotys for the victims and their families. Although the government tried seventy-eight workers, only about twenty remained in prison by May, 1977. At the same time that it released fourteen of the group, the regime charged bourgeois ideological sabotage against their defenders. Human rights advocates were arrested, kept in jail for a few days, and released after questioning. Then they were rearrested a week or so later.

Two Cities

Postwar Poland can be best understood by looking at two cities: Warsaw in the North and Cracow in the South. Warsaw was almost totally destroyed in World War II as the Nazis attempted to extinguish Polish culture. Its rebellious citizens were massacred by the thousands. Russian troops delayed coming while the Nazis systematically demolished the city. Today, Warsaw is remarkably restored: the old Market Square, the Cardinal's Church, the old palace of the Polish kings. Men and women are dressed attractively, in spite of a lack of consumer goods. The many books published annually include a long religious list; they are an index of cultural life.

Cracow belonged to the old Austro-Hungarian empire. Once the capital of the old Polish kingdom, it was spared destruction in the war. The city boasts the largest medieval market square in Europe. Its century-old churches remain, together with the university where the astronomer Copernicus worked. Poland gave religious freedom to Jews and Protestants while religious wars raged in Western Europe. A Polish army rescued Vienna from the Turks in 1683. Little more than a hundred years later, Polish territory was divided between Austria, Prussia, and Russia.

Poles longed for nationhood throughout the nineteenth century. Their independence was given back after World War I, only to be destroyed by the Nazis. Today a deep sense of national loyalty joins all parts of the population in concern for national survival. Most of all, Poles are patriots.

Student Protest

The student festival of Juvenalia is celebrated annually in mid-May at Cracow with costumes, parades, and dancing. In 1977, it was abruptly terminated by the students themselves, following the death of one of them, Stanislav Pyjas.[14] Instead of joining a mummy parade, they stood with black flags before his house. Some of the signs read "Murder!" In Warsaw, 730 students had signed petitions asking for investigation of Radom and Ursus. Another 285 at the Catholic University of Lublin had signed.

Stanislav Pyjas was a philosophy student. Politically active, he had collected 517 signatures in Cracow. After his protest to the state attorney he received threatening, anonymous letters.

His battered body was found at the foot of the stairs in the house where he lived on Zweweska Street. The police report said he had 2.6 parts per thousand alcohol in his blood and had fallen down drunk. His fellow students did not believe the account, and five thousand of them marched with candles and black arm bands to honor his memory. The procession moved from the Dominican Church to the National Cathedral where the Polish kings lie buried.

Arrested among the student committee protestors was Adam Michnik. In an open letter he wrote:

> I will cry out. As my friends expected, I was arrested. I do not know whether I and my friends arrested with me will be released or not, and this time be held longer behind bars. I do not know yet whether and under what charges they will seek to convict me: espionage for the Australians or supposed work with the secret service from Venezuela. What I do know is that the true reason for my arrest and perhaps my punishment is: I shall be punished because I am not in agreement. I do not agree to recognize a principle in which man is the state's property and the state belongs to the ruling power elite. I refuse to remain quiet about the wrong done against people in my country. . . . This is the moral reason for my action; as long as community relations in my country are based on lies, I will not keep quiet. I will cry out because this is the only thing I can do. I will cry out because this is the only possible witness that enables me behind bars still to remain a man. I will cry out because I believe in the future of my land and my people.[15]

Testimony before the U.S. Congressional Commission on Security and Cooperation in Europe included this statement: "As far as freedom of conscience is concerned, everyone in Poland is free, and for this purpose no resolution of the Helsinki Conference was necessary."[16] Yet many people do act contrary to their consciences, informing against each other. And the secret police use torture. "By law freedom of religion is guaranteed." Yet in Poland today, a practicing Roman Catholic's chances for professional advancement are like those of an atheist in the Vatican. Freedom of thought is guaranteed on the statute books, but there are constant obstacles. Meetings of the Workers' Defense Committee are regularly raided by the police. News from abroad is censored. A citizen who is out of favor with authorities is refused permission to travel. The right to work is constantly violated. The testimony concluded: "By signing the Final Act of the Helsinki Conference, the Polish Government committed itself once again to respect human rights. But the principles of Helsinki will have a positive influence on the situation in Europe only if any government's violations of human rights is publicly and unequivocally denounced by other signatory nations."[17]

The Church

Before his arrest, Adam Michnik completed a book on the relation of the church to intellectuals in his country.[18] He gave particular attention to the lot of secular persons who wish to find a middle way between Marxism and Catholicism. Communist totalitarian strategy has forced virtually all such persons toward the side of the church, which has not overtly encouraged (much less solicited) this movement; still it has remained the defender of national identity. In this role, human rights and freedom to worship God have coalesced. Roman Catholic leadership has been careful not to become an agency for external foreign policy.

Much of the strength of the Roman Catholic church has come from the leadership of Cardinal Wyszynski. Released from imprisonment in 1956, he initiated the celebration of a millenium of Christianity in Poland, 966–1966. The church is in effect the protector of human rights. Attendance and participation in the church in Poland averages at least 70 percent.

The Roman Catholic church has not always been a progressive institution. Apologists admit its defensiveness to change in the last century and even in the era of independence.[19] Yet today it remains the one place where there is freedom of opinion in a totalitarian state. Clergy do not receive state stipends, as they do in a number of other East European countries. The freewill offerings of the faithful support not only churches, but the only Roman Catholic university in any Communist land, at Lublin, Poland. Intellectuals as well as workers honor the church.

The matter was summed up cogently by a ranking Roman Catholic official. "Without the Russian Communist pressure," he said, "our churches would be as empty as those in France. But when a Pole considers the Russian occupation after World War II and the closeness of the Russian border, a chill goes up and down his spine. He moves toward the church." The official knew his comment was an oversimplification. Yet it has truth. A large part of the Polish clergy, Roman Catholic and Protestant, suffered martyrdom in World War II. Poland's new national saint, Father Kolbe, gave up his life in exchange for that of a family man when the Nazis were executing hostages.

East Germany

Whereas Poland has been a Roman Catholic country, East Germany has been traditionally Protestant. It was the home of Martin Luther and the heartland of the Reformation. Compared with Poland, the Communist state has been effective in creating a very different situation. Church attendance is low. There is not a crystallization of national sentiment as in its Eastern neighbor. Only one Poland exists, but there are two Germanys.

East Germany, under Russian sponsorship, has developed only with difficulty a separate identity and loyalty. A significant part of the population migrated to West Germany before the building of the Berlin Wall. More than Poland, East Germany is open to penetration by radio and television from the West. Its citizens live in two worlds, that of their own work and city during the day, and that of a far richer Germany in the West which can be seen on the television screen each night.

The aim of the East German government is to develop a totally secular society that excludes religion. This is evident in the state confirmation service which has replaced church confirmation. Also, whole busloads of school children can be seen on German freeways on Sunday mornings being taken for excursions on this particular day so their parents will not be tempted to send them to church.

St. Thomas Church in Leipzig, where J.S. Bach's oratorios were first performed, was not destroyed in the bombings of World War II. Its famous boys' choir still sings each Sunday morning from the choir loft. Whereas other churches have very small congregations, some three to four hundred people gather in the St. Thomas sanctuary each week.

The officiating minister wears a high, starched, pleated collar. "I do not tell you that you must have your children confirmed," he says. "There may well be difficulties at work, perhaps even in the family. But if this is your conviction, then fulfill your Christian responsibility." The proclamation is made in the knowledge that everyone attending comes at risk to his person, his job, and educational discrimination — the threat of second-class citizenship.

Another pastor, Oscar Brüsewitz, drove onto the square at Zeitz, August 18, 1976. Pouring gasoline on himself, he set it aflame, inflicting wounds which led to his death.[20] The question of whether such a protest is allowable on Christian grounds need not destroy his message: a protest against the fact that religion is being systematically withheld from young people. Those who remain alive wish only basic human rights, not special privileges.

Fourteen months later in October, 1977, a thousand students demonstrated during a government celebration in East Berlin, crying out for the Russians to leave.[21] As much as a concern for human rights, nationalism is a major sentiment in Eastern Europe. Germany, unlike Poland, is a divided land, part of a nation that suffered defeat in World War II. The Communists know the Lutheran state church long supported German nationalism, a sentiment they have every reason to fear. The desires to worship God freely and to determine the nation's own destiny touch deep bases of motivation and feeling.

Of course, the closer one comes to Eastern Europe the more dangerous the issue of human rights becomes. Members of the Swiss General Staff released a paper appraising the situation during the first Belgrade review of the Helsinki accord. Part of the importance of the document lies in the fact that it comes from a neutral land long committed to democracy. The generals acknowledge positively that Western interest in human rights has led to ideological gains. However, they note it has not lessened Russian repression in East Berlin, Prague, or Warsaw. The overbearing Soviet need for security, the paper concludes, will cause Moscow to regard every movement for freedom in the USSR or satellite lands as a threat. "A certain care from the side of the West is recommended."

It is important to recognize that Russia is practicing a form of colonialism that has been given up elsewhere. Militarily, the satellite countries form a buffer zone for the Soviets. Culturally, however, Moscow has not had success. Citizens of their East European allies look overwhelmingly to the West for their model. The situation is not a static one. Nor can the issue of human rights be avoided as Communist regimes seek economic benefits from contact with the West while continuing ideological struggle and forbidding free personal contact. The defensiveness is on the side of the Communists. The West has nothing to lose by openness and an exchange of ideas and persons.

4

What Jimmy Carter Has/Has Not Done

Less than a month after President Carter's inauguration, a Russian scientist was invited to the American Embassy on Tchaikovsky Street in Moscow. A tall, stoop-shouldered man entered and was shown into the office of a ranking Embassy official. The nuclear physicist had been the foremost designer of the Russian atomic bomb. Today he no longer holds any official post. As a leader of the Russian dissidents, he had written both candidates during the presidential campaign. Then he wrote to Carter on the day after his inauguration, asking the American to "raise his voice" on behalf of prisoners of conscience in Eastern Europe. The letter was on Carter's desk, awaiting a policy decision, immediately after he came to office. Andrei Sakharov was given Carter's reply at the American Embassy:

I received your letter of January 21, and I want to express my appreciation to you for bringing your thoughts to my personal attention. Human rights is a central concern of my administration. . . . We shall use our good offices to seek the release of prisoners of conscience, and we will continue our effort to shape a world responsive to human aspirations in which nations of different cultures and histories can live side by side in peace and justice.

I am always glad to hear from you and I wish you well.[1]

Human rights was an issue which could not be avoided. Few Americans understood President Ford's reasons for refusing to invite Alexander Solzhenitsyn to the White House. Carter avoided this mistake, but had he made another? Was his reply a futile gesture which could prove counterproductive in the long run? Professor Hans J. Morgenthau observed that nothing like this had happened since Gladstone rose up against Disraeli to protest the atrocities in Bulgaria. No other American president had intervened in the internal affairs of other countries in defense of their people's human rights. "It is terribly naive; it is well-intentioned, but it is immature."[2] He added: "It is nonsense, and it won't do anybody any good." For Carter's policy to work, he maintained, a moralistic American state would have to take over the whole world.

What can or should the United States do about dissidents? The Kremlin would like to increase economic and scientific exchange with the West without "interference in its domestic affairs." Yet its repression, including the misuse of psychiatry, cannot be ignored. Russian news media daily castigate capitalism, yet they raise loud protest—even alleging that détente is imperiled—when Western voices speak out in defense of human rights. Moscow continues to intervene militarily in places like Ethiopia and Angola.

The President's Foreign Affairs Advisor denied that Carter had acted impulsively. Informed observers cite evidence that the Kremlin had been preparing strong measures against the dissidents even before Carter came to office.[3] Sakharov himself seems to have felt in danger and might have been arrested had it not been for the President's words. Most of the dissidents believe repression would have come with or without Carter's writing.

The response in the Russian press showed that the President had raised a central issue. Yuri Kornilov, a senior commentator for the government news agency, wrote for *Tass*: "James Carter has assumed the role of mentor to the

USSR and other socialist countries, using the most ludicrous and wild concoctions borrowed from the stock in trade of reactionary bourgeois propaganda."[4]

Sakharov commented, "I do not believe that President Carter intends to step away from his principled position on human rights. If he were to do this, it would be a catastrophe on a world scale."[5]

The Debate About
Carter's New Emphasis

In his inaugural address Carter reflected:

> I have just taken the oath of office on the Bible my mother gave me a few years ago, opened to a timeless admonition from the ancient prophet Micah: "He hath showed thee, O man, what is good; and what doth the Lord require of thee, but to do justly, and to love mercy, and to walk humbly with thy God."
>
> . . . To be true to ourselves, we must be true to others.
>
> Because we are free we can never be indifferent to the fate of freedom elsewhere. Our moral sense dictates a clear-cut preference for those societies which share with us an abiding respect for individual human rights. We do not seek to intimidate, but it is clear that a world which others can dominate with impunity would be inhospitable to decency.[6]

Carter's concern for human rights has been projected worldwide. The President has been characterized as a "moralist fighting unrighteousness from Quitman County, Georgia, to Uganda . . . a planning and fixing President . . . strong-willed . . . striving to make the world rearrange itself in accord with higher standards—the ambitious, practical, victorious, punctual, healthy-minded. . . ."[7] This is the opinion of Professor William Lee Miller of Indiana University, who adds that Carter may well be the most intelligent man to run for president in modern times.

"In attempting to place human rights at the center of his

foreign policy, Jimmy Carter has got hold of an idea that is very powerful but also very complex."[8] Such was the conclusion of a reporter-at-large for the *New Yorker* magazine after a series of interviews with officials in Washington. Human rights not only means different things to different people, said the reporter, but it involves the United States in the most sensitive internal affairs of other nations and runs the risk of colliding with other foreign policy aims—peace, détente, and world order.

A critic urges that the President's inauguration espousal of an "absolute" commitment to human rights was an overstatement. A promise, the critic says, to do all we can to protect them would have been more in keeping with the image of humility and subdued realism that Carter carefully cultivated during his campaign for office. At the same time, however, the critic acknowledges that "the vow of absolutism may have reflected spiritual zeal, but it is as probable that it expressed an audacious political genius."[9]

International Relations

The President has been seeking international support. Addressing the United Nations General Assembly early in his administration, Carter noted:

> All the signatories of the U.N. Charter have pledged themselves to observe and to respect basic human rights. Thus, no member of the United Nations can claim that mistreatment of its citizens is solely its own business. Equally, no member can avoid its responsibilities to review and to speak when torture or unwarranted deprivation occurs in any part of the world.
>
> The basic thrust of human affairs points toward a more universal demand for fundamental human rights. . . . Ours is a commitment, and not just a political posture.[10]

A variety of voices have warned against a missionary effort to impose American patterns on all mankind—a new crusade to "make the world safe for democracy." Kennedy biographer and historian Arthur Schlesinger has called Carter a "narcissistic loner with fixations of righteousness."[11]

Carter's defense of human rights has been a deliberate strategy, the goal of which has been to create an ethos and interest which will favor personal freedom and justice. In this, he was initially successful. During visits to the White House, heads of government reported the release of political prisoners in their countries. But in spite of such gains, the question remains as to how much an American president can alter political structures by proclamation. Will his sense of justice restrain brute power? Can high motive and purpose be effective in today's world?

Deputy Secretary of State Warren Christopher pointed out to Carter critics that the Chief Executive is attempting to "restore confidence both at home and abroad."[12] The issue is not just what kind of a foreign policy the United States will have; it concerns what kind of a president and what kind of a country there will be. The fundamental need, in Christopher's judgment, is to establish an entire governmental structure that will regain the confidence and backing of the public that has been lost since Vietnam and Watergate.

History

The fact is that the United States' support for human rights has been only sporadic in the past. In the immediate postwar period, the Truman and Eisenhower administrations were committed to international responsibility. By 1953, however, serious implementation of human rights had faltered in the face of congressional opposition led by Senator Bricker.[13] Even the United Nation's treaty outlawing genocide—the mass murder of whole peoples— remained unratified. President Kennedy attempted to arouse idealism again, but without effective results. Subsequently, American concern turned to the war in Vietnam.

Secretary of State Kissinger's concern for détente and the end of hostilities in Southeast Asia left little place for human rights.

Initially, Carter's campaign for human rights put the Russians on the defensive. It is evident that human rights are more respected in the Western democracies than elsewhere. Those who do not have them look to the West for help and inspiration, not to Moscow. Carter and his advisors do not believe the West is declining nor that Moscow can in the foreseeable future close the technology gap. Working from a conservative, bureaucratic base, the USSR is not keeping pace with the West economically. In the Third World it is losing ideological appeal. The United States need not panic, attempting to strike a bargain quickly before conditions change for the worse.

In a second address at the United Nations, during the fall of 1977, Carter was less outspoken about human rights, yet he did not retreat from the issue. To emphasize its importance, he signed the two U.N. covenants on political and economic rights. These documents still await ratification by the U.S. Senate before the nation can participate fully in the United Nation's international monitoring of human rights.

Brzezinski: The Technetronic Revolution

Zbigniew Brzezinski has replaced Henry Kissinger as chief presidential advisor for foreign affairs and head of the National Security Council. This specialist's long-term analysis of international relations is of crucial importance to Carter's thinking. Brzezinski has written about Japan and Africa. Most importantly, he is an authority on Russia and Eastern Europe. *Between Two Ages* is his most comprehensive theoretical book.[14] Carter is reported to have read it a number of times. Brzezinski argues that the most advanced countries, led by the United States, have passed from the industrial stage of development to what he calls the technetronic age.

Values and social structures are being radically changed by new technology, especially electronics. In fact, the impact of the technetronic age is worldwide. Concretely visible in terms of hydrogen bombs, mass communication, and computers, it alters weapons, ideology, and economics on a global basis. For statecraft, it means international politics no longer can center only on relatively self-contained, homogeneous nations.

The industrial revolution shifted life-styles from a primarily agricultural pattern to factory and city ways. Now, automation and cybernetics are displacing this arrangement. Individual workers are of less and less importance. Technology is only one of a variety of factors that contribute to economic depersonalization and lack of cohesion in life. The hope that science would unify communities or enhance personal existence has not been fulfilled. Life is more and more fragmented even as the world draws closer together spatially. Brzezinski maintains that problems other societies will confront later are already highly visible in the United States. What seems to be emerging is not a global village. Instead, the global city is nervous, agitated, and tense—a fragmented web of interdependent relations.

The United States is the principal disseminator of the technetronic revolution. It is the most innovative and creative society. Simply by being itself, it is a major disruptive influence on the world scene. America's technology, rather than its ideals, engenders dynamic innovation. A large part of the world learns about its own future by looking at the United States. Brzezinski sees America's relationship with the rest of the world as intimate, porous, and complex. It evokes global attention, emulation, envy, admiration, and animosity.

Communism capitalizes on the aspirations and frustrations that change brings. Many countries in the Third World have yet to undergo the industrial revolution. Anarchy, racialism, and extreme nationalism root in feelings of psychological deprivation, not just in poverty alone. Liberty has little meaning amid poverty. The subjective revolution that precedes economic change in underdeveloped countries creates anger, unrest, and outrage.

Brzezinski argues that an anti-Communist strategy is not enough. The need to overcome technological backwardness, eliminate poverty, prevent overpopulation, and extend international cooperation in education and health spheres is urgent. Foreign policy must be responsive, both to more traditional political problems and to new issues. It must combine "power realism" with "planetary humanism." An interplay of utopian goals and practical steps is called for.

Brzezinski believes the history of the United States involves such a relationship. He sees it as a peculiar blend of aristocratic tradition, constitutional legalism, and mass democracy. Only occasionally have these traditions clashed, as in the Civil War when aristocracy suffered.By and large, the American democratic tradition has provided a humane framework for creative problem-solving. What causes the present stress and strain? Brzezinski lists three reasons for the decline of American foreign influence under Secretary of State Kissinger: the predilection for (1) the personal over the politic, (2) the covert over the conceptual, and (3) the acrobatic over the architectural.[15]

In an article in a popular magazine—"Unmanifest Destiny: Where Do We Go from Here?"—Brzezinski stressed the negative effect of a dominant pessimistic outlook in large sectors of Western societies.[16] The phenomenon is all the more dangerous today because much of the initiative for grand-scale global relations in a technetronic world must necessarily come from the United States. A democracy rests not on institutions or economic arrangements but on people's beliefs. Thus, the erosion of its core beliefs is highly destructive. Brzezinski calls for a universal humanism that will shape a world community.

A New Humanism

Why has such a humanism not been forthcoming? Brzezinski finds that part of the explanation is an overload of the democratic system, an overflow of information that has been difficult for the public and legislators to assimilate. But this is only part of the cause. Brzezinski insists that what society needs most of all in a time of transition is a definition of principles, an affirmation of convictions, and a willingness to act on devotion to ideals. "A society that does not believe in anything," he says, "is a society in a state of dissolution."[17]

Carter's Christian commitment has provided a faith basis. Speaking to a visitor in the Oval Office, he said:

> So we have some things, our religious beliefs and the ideal of what our government ought to be, that are stabilizing forces. And I think that this is not incompatible with historical trends. There comes a time in a crisis when the superb qualities of human beings in a collective fashion are evoked in a religious concept or in a governmental structure that transcends the mundane commitments of people. But it stands there then as a reminder of what people can do.[18]

Referring to Reinhold Niebuhr, the Christian theologian he cites most often, Carter explained:

> Government is what the laws are and . . . there's an almost perfect concept expressed in the Christian ethic, that there's an ultimate pattern for government, but the struggle to reach it is always unsuccessful. The perfect standard is one that human beings don't quite reach, but we try to.[19]

Political considerations are, no doubt, involved in Carter's campaign for human rights. But this campaign has also been an expression of his own faith commitments. Procedural democracy alone does not supply the necessary principles or conviction. This is the point at which Carter's religious concern becomes relevant to human rights.

Civil liberties, however imperfectly realized, have been a fundamental tenet of the American republic for more than two hundred years. Unusual conditions have produced the present crisis with its worldwide repercussions. The war in Vietnam evoked bitter self-examination in millions of Americans. It became clear that simple anticommunism was not a satisfactory principle of foreign policy amid the complexities of the modern world. The Watergate scandal raised serious concerns about public morals at home. Yet these factors alone did not produce a new outlook. A specific catalyst was needed. It came from a Southern governor deeply committed to civil rights.

Brzezinski remarks that the United States has set higher standards for itself than any other society. Carter's politics reflect this concern. He understands that America's relationship to the world must reflect its domestic values and interests. A profound discrepancy between external conduct and internal norms is no longer possible. Mass communication exposes and debilitates support needed for foreign policy in the face of such schizophrenia.

Evaluation

Criticism of America's long-term role needs to be taken seriously. Whether negative claims are accepted or rejected, they should be considered. President Wilson injected moral idealism into the power struggle of World War I. In the end, his plan for a League of Nations was rejected by his countrymen and a repressive peace imposed on Germany by the Treaty of Versailles. Had America remained involved with Europe, World War II might have been avoided. The United States again joined hostilities in 1941, and subsequently, critics charged that Roosevelt surrendered half of Europe to Stalin at Yalta. Later, American idealism again asserted itself in Vietnam. When the United States withdrew, hundreds of thousands of its supporters were left to suffer.

The long-term question remains: How can human rights be supported nationally or internationally? Nationalism— intense loyalty to country even to the point of absolute devotion—is among the most powerful forces in the modern world. Governments claim absolute sovereignty and the right of self-determination. Do they have authority to act in any way they please? Interdependent in economics and technology, they still seek to remain independent politically. Should they be entitled to treat their citizens as they wish? Who has the right of self-determination: the oppressor or the oppressed?

A friendly commentator says the President's emphasis on human rights is no accident. "Carter chose the theme with premeditation, with a little guile, and with a good deal of conviction."[20] Conceptually, it is a little Wilsonian. "In practice, it is pure Jimmy Carter."

The same commentator describes three risks inherent in Carter's policy: (1) the risk that the human rights crusade will adversely effect negotiations with the USSR and other nations; (2) the risk that if the United States insists on human rights, it cannot keep countries like South Korea and the Philippines as allies; and (3) most importantly, the risk that the United States will be unsuccessful in any move from an arrogance of power to an arrogance of conscience.

Carter as a Moralist

It has been charged that Carter is a second Woodrow Wilson, directing foreign policy from a Christian pulpit.[21] Can he talk about human rights without committing an "indecent, self-righteous act?" Joseph Duffey, assistant secretary of state for cultural affairs, answers that Carter can because the President has a strong sense of the problems of pride.[22] One of Carter's most perceptive interpreters has been Garry Wills, a Roman Catholic. He finds that Carter's religiosity is personal, not a public righteousness.[23] In fact, Woodrow Wilson denied the very limits Carter emphasizes.

Wills argues that, retrospectively, it is clear that Wilson wanted to impose a virtuous Americanism on the world. By contrast, Carter has coupled his denunciation of repressive measures elsewhere with extraordinary presidential admissions of American failures. As a Southerner, Carter comes from a region that has known both defeat and guilt. In fact, he made a dramatic confession of Southern wrongdoing when, as governor of Georgia, he hung the portrait of Martin Luther King, Jr. in the state capitol. Wills maintains that Carter does not talk about good automatically succeeding, nor does he share the illusion of inevitable progress. His optimism is tempered by both realism and religion.

As governor of Georgia, Wills points out that Carter had to relate to and deal with a variety of people implicated in the vast evil of racism. He did so, while at the same time maintaining his condemnation of their violations of human rights. Now, as president, he has asked Congress to allow him to be "flexible" in dealing with important allies guilty of repressive policies. Critics note he is harder on some offenders than on others. Wills's answer is that Carter's policy is not inconsistent; it is plain, simple morality. The President refuses to press his human rights policy in some cases because he knows that in certain instances this would exacerbate the problem.

Carter does not subscribe to the schematization of the world into "us" and "them" as did Wilson. Wills argues that Wilson defined as virtuous anyone who would receive him or defer to him, thus dividing the world neatly into two camps. Such ideological polarity is absent in Carter; rather, he denounces evil whenever and wherever he can. He calls for respect for human rights in his own country as well as abroad.

Carter is prepared to meet with all comers! At the same time, the President invokes the notion of basic decency like a Southern schoolmarm, speaking of what "good folk" do. Like all moral men, he is limited by the need to survive in a sinful world. Wills feels it is precisely this recognition of limits that distinguishes his outlook from "the illusions of modernity." Carter knows it is nonsense to think we have nothing to fear but fear itself. We have evil to fear. Recognition of its presence prompts his unconventionally fervent talk of eliminating nuclear weapons.

The New World of Jimmy Carter

In fact, Carter's policy is one of conviction and not simply one of expediency. His speech at Notre Dame University in the spring of 1977 was a carefully-thought-out policy statement. Addressing the class of 1977, he said:

> We live in a world that is imperfect and will always be imperfect, a world that is complex and will always be complex. I understand fully the limits of moral suasion. I have no illusion that changes come easily or soon. But I also believe that it is a mistake to undervalue the power of words and of the ideas that words embody. In our own history that power has ranged from Thomas Paine's "Common Sense" to Martin Luther King, Jr.'s "I Have a Dream."
>
> In the life of the human spirit, words are action—much more than many of us may realize who live in countries where freedom of expression is taken for granted.
>
> The leaders of the totalitarian countries understand this very well. The proof is that words are precisely the action for which the dissidents in those countries are being persecuted.[24]

Carter identified the essential differences between the world in which he must make policy decisions and the old world of his presidential predecessors. In the old world, the United States attempted to contain Soviet expansion by an "almost exclusive alliance among non-Communist nations." Carter acknowledged that "an inordinate fear of Communism . . . led us to embrace any dictator who joined us in our fear." In the black-and-white world where being Communist or anti-Communist was the only important factor in international relations, there was little place for human rights in American diplomacy. A land or dictator had only to be anti-Communist in order to receive help from the United States. The Notre Dame speech made plain that this policy is no longer in force. Instead, the President spoke of reaching out to developing nations "to alleviate suffering and to reduce the chasm between the world's rich and poor." Idealism alone is not the only factor; Third World countries are important suppliers of raw materials.

President Carter did not destroy the old world single-handedly. Long before he came to office, the Prague Spring, the Russian dissidents, Amnesty International, and American congressional concern had begun the struggle. Not limiting foreign policy to communism vs. anticommunism, Carter has added the human rights dimension. Joseph C. Harsch, writing in the *Christian Science Monitor*, remarked, "Mr. Carter is now moving into a new world with new problems and new priorities. The journey will be an interesting one."[25]

Andrei Amalrik was asked about his view of President Carter's policy on human rights. "I am very pleased with it indeed," he replied, but added that it is much too early to evaluate it.[26] "The trouble with Americans is that they always expect immediate results." Amalrik emphasized that the Carter administration must be firm and patient. "It must not let itself be swayed either by the current reactions of the Soviet regime or by the discomfiture and alarm of its Western European allies, or indeed, by public opinion, which fails to understand that the Soviet regime is not going to change its policies, mildly or drastically, overnight." Why the concern over American pressure, Amalrik asked. The U.S. government "has simply voiced its concern, and has made it known to Moscow that its oppressive policies will not go unnoticed." Amalrik concluded: "What Carter is saying now is long overdue. His policy is both morally just and, in addition, politically sagacious."

5

Stalinism and Eurocommunism

A new group of young French philosophers, shocked by exposés of Stalin's Gulag Archipelago, has concluded that communism is an obsolete ideology which leads inevitably to totalitarianism.[1] Its promises to bring real change are empty. The state has not withered away as Marx predicted. Instead, it has grown into a monstrous "reactionary machine" which can lead to world catastrophe. Turning away from the search for ideological systems, this new group expresses concern for personal ethics and moral duty.

Are these anti-Marxists too inclusive in their indictment? Communists continue to champion revolution, not reform. Communists hold that the larger movement of history is more important than the individual. Human rights need not be respected for the bourgeois or older established classes. Those rights have been created by the regime, and they are class privileges reserved for persons who share in the dictatorship of the proletariat. Was Marx naive in predicting the disappearance of the state? What is the relation between Marx, Lenin, and Stalin?

The Russian Revolution

The Winter Palace in Leningrad was stormed during the early hours of November 8, 1917. At 2:10 A.M., soldiers, sailors, and workers penetrated to the Hall of Mirrors where the Provisional Government was assembled. On behalf of the Communist Revolutionary Military Committee, Antonov-Ovseyenko announced, "I declare you, the members of the Provisional Government, under arrest."[2] The deputy premier of the last non-Communist Russian government conceded, "The members of the Provisional Government yield to force and surrender to avoid bloodshed."[3] A dozen years earlier, in 1905, Tsarist soldiers had fired on a crowd of people protesting before the Winter Palace. A large number of persons, many clutching holy pictures and crucifixes, had been killed. Now, all such religious appeals for help were derogated.

"Give us an organization of revolutionaries, and we will overturn Russia,"[4] wrote Lenin as he developed a party of professional revolutionaries, rigorously disciplined in a way Marx had never envisaged. John Reed, an American reporter, described the scene on the evening of November 8: "Lenin, dressed in shabby clothes, his trousers much too long for him, addressed his fellow Bolsheviks, gripping the edge of the reading stand, letting his little winking eyes travel over the crowd as he stood there, waiting, apparently oblivious to the long, rolling ovation, which lasted several minutes. When it finished, he said simply, 'We shall now proceed to construction of the socialist order.' "[5]

Today, Lenin's face "stares down from countless portraits, gazes out from ten-ruble bank notes, strides boldly or sits contemplatively in statuary halls, squares, parks, and museums from one end of the country to the other."[6] He is the secular saint of the USSR. Lenin is eulogized as a genius, the "great," the "immortal," and described as "more alive than the living." His picture is in every office and he receives hero worship in cantatas, oratorios, plays, novels, films, and on television. No doubt he was a brilliant, energetic revolutionary, a strategist and improviser. Personally kind, he was the unlooser of political terror.

According to Marx, the dictatorship of the proletariat was to be a transitional phase on the road to a classless society. The police were to be stripped of their political power and the organs of the state would no longer be masters of society, but its servants. Lenin, in contrast, explained, "The dictatorship presupposes the ruthlessly severe, swift, and resolute use of force to crush the resistance of the exploiters, the capitalists, landowners, and their underlings. Whoever does not understand this is not a revolutionary and must be removed from the post of leader or adviser of the proletariat."[7]

Freedom

Rosa Luxemburg, a German Communist, was outspoken in criticism of Lenin's theory and actions: "Without general elections, without unrestricted freedom of the press and assembly, without a free struggle of opinion, life goes out in any public institution, becomes a mere semblance of life, in which only the bureaucracy remains as the active element. Public life gradually falls asleep. . . ."[8]

In May of 1842, six years before the Communist Manifesto, Karl Marx wrote, "The essence of a free press is the principled, reasonable, moral essence of freedom. The character of a censored press is the unprincipled aberration of unfreedom; it is a civilized abomination, a perfumed monster."[9] He pointed out further that censorship is based on the principle that the end justifies the means, "but an end which requires unjustifiable means is not a justifiable end."[10] Marx was only twenty-four years old when he argued this way while working for a newly founded newspaper, the *Rheinische Zeitung* in Cologne, Germany. He concluded, "A censored press has a demoralizing effect. . . . The government only hears its own voice, yet it persists in the delusion that it hears the voice of the people and in turn demands of the people that they should persist in this delusion."[11]

Marx's followers have not established freedom of the press. Why not? The oppression of workers and the censorship he protested were ruthless. Yet his dialectical materialism leaves little place for human rights except as class privileges. Unlike the men of the Enlightenment, Marx argued that morality is not timeless; it is the product of economic and social conditions. When the economic organization of society is changed, man himself will be reformed. In the preface to his *Critique of Political Economy*, he set out his basic premise:

> The mode of production of material life conditions the social, political, and intellectual life process in general. It is not the consciousness of men that determines their being, but, on the contrary, their social being that determines their consciousness.[12]

In Marx's "scientific socialism" there are no eternal values. Law and ethics turn on economic forces and circumstances. The founder of communism expected revolution—at times by violence, at times by parliamentary means. Marx claimed to be scientific. But science—which he mistakenly interpreted as materialistic—provides no guarantees for human dignity. Rather, it is the product of man's intelligence and freedom. In the demand for revolution, Marx compromised unyielding respect for the rights of man. Man must change the world, overcoming tyranny. There are no transcendent moral values, according to Marx. In fact, there is nothing beyond material forms and processes.

Naturalism, Humanism, Theism

At least three alternatives need to be identified in considering the Communist position: naturalism, humanism, and theism. The first allows only the natural, material world. Classical humanism distinguishes man and nature more drastically, claiming that human reason and freedom cannot be explained from the belief that man is only a natural being. Theism—belief in a personal God—includes three realities in ascending order of importance: nature, man, and God.

Marx believed that older naturalisms had understood the universe in too static a fashion. He borrowed the notion of dialectic—a dynamic movement embracing opposites—from the German philosopher Georg Friedrich Hegel. Whereas Hegel's dialectic was one of spirit, Marx's reference was matter.

Professor Robert Tucker of Princeton University argues that Hegel had given up the notion of a personal deity.[13] Marx's criticism was directed more against Hegel's grandiose system than against the God of the Bible. However this may be, religion according to Marx is only the "opiate of the people," absolutizing the status quo in a timeless world. What was formerly explained by religious mythology—the creation of the world, for example—can now be explained scientifically in the course of nature. According to naturalism, biological evolution has shown that man is not made in the image of God; man makes God in his own image. But can such naturalism account for freedom and human rights?

Marx's view has been labeled reductionistic by its critics; it describes only part of reality. Marx wrote his doctoral thesis on Greek philosophy. He knew that the orientation of thinkers like Socrates and Plato was not naturalistic but humanistic. These philosophers found that nature by itself provides no explanation for value or meaning, much less conscience. They gave up looking for an explanation in the physical universe alone, concluding that thought and spirit are radically different from matter.

Humanism distinguishes between man and nature, emphasizing the unique experience of reason and freedom. On this basis, human rights can be defended as they cannot in naturalism. They are not just class privileges, as contemporary Marxists allege; they have their justification from a higher law or reason.

Theism, belief in a personal God, is even less acceptable in communism. Marx agreed with his contemporary Ludwig Feuerbach that religion reflects only the agony and suffering of mankind and the world. The same can be said of any religiously based ethic. There is no ultimate except nature. The question is whether respect for a higher law is necessary to civil liberties. Naturalism cannot explain human dignity, much less provide motivation for it.

Marxism is not simply a view of reality; it is also a program of action for the future which promises hope—a new age with a changed humanity. Lacking any intrinsic values, its hopes are exclusively this-worldly. To date they have not been realized. Human rights were increasingly downgraded in the succession of Communist leadership from Marx to Lenin to Stalin.

Stalinism

Before Lenin died in 1924, he had come to suspect Stalin. The latter suppressed Lenin's will and ruthlessly made his way to absolute dictatorship. Stalin's show trials began in 1936. Lenin's closest comrades were defamed as murderers, rabid dogs, fascist lackeys, monsters, the scum of humanity, and a gang of the people's enemies—and they were destroyed.

Khrushchev denounced his predecessor at the Twentieth Party Congress in 1956, acknowledging that mass repression had been justified by the term "enemy of the people."

This term made possible the usage of the most cruel repression, violating all norms of revolutionary legality, against anyone who in any way disagreed with Stalin, against those who were only suspected of hostile intent, against those who had bad reputations. . . . The only proof of guilt used, against all current norms of legal science, was the "confession" of the accused himself; and, as subsequent probing proved, "confessions" were acquired through physical pressure against the accused.[14]

Communism provided no moral bases for reform. No real attempt was made to destroy Stalinist totalitarianism; the excesses of the system were merely reduced and curbed. Party bureaucrats resisted Khrushchev's reforms. On October 15, 1964, he was deposed.

Humanist Marxism

The thoroughgoing rejection of Stalinism, both in theory and practice, came from outside Russia. Influenced by nationalism, Czechoslovakian leadership set out on an independent road to socialism, attacking bureaucracy and statism. Marxist philosopher Karel Kosik wrote during the Prague Spring:

> The cause of our political crisis lies in the fact that citizens of this country no longer want to live as a Party or non-Party mass without rights, or with inadequate rights, and that the exponents of power are no longer able to assert their leading role in a police-type bureaucratic dictatorship.[15]

The Prague Spring became a general reform movement. Party leaders virtually overnight relaxed censorship of press, television, and radio. Criticism of past crimes aroused new political interest and hope, an intensity of activity unknown during the past years. In addition to critical analysis of Stalinist abuse of human rights, including the show trials in Czechoslovakia, the conviction emerged that such a state of affairs should never be allowed to happen again.

The Action Program of the Central Committee was set forth on April 10, 1968:

> Socialist state power cannot be monopolized either by a single

party or by a coalition of parties. It must be open to all political organizations of the people. . . . Constitutional freedoms of assembly and association must be ensured this year so that the possibility of setting up voluntary organizations, special interest associations, societies, etc., is guaranteed by law and the present interests and needs of various strata and categories of our citizens are taken care of without bureaucratic interference and without a monopoly by any individual organization.[16]

During the night of August 20, 1968, Czechoslovakia was occupied by Soviet troops, supported by those of East Germany, Poland, Hungary, and Bulgaria.

Eurocommunism

Today, the contemporary movement known as Eurocommunism has not entirely accepted the Czechoslovakian reformers' outlook. Yet Western Communist party leaders have found it increasingly difficult to ignore the abuse of human rights in Eastern Europe. The name Eurocommunism refers to the parties of Western Europe which have become more and more separated from Russian domination, in particular, in Italy, France, and Spain. It is not a fully unified movement. West European Communist leaders cannot hope to win votes in elections on totalitarian bases. It was the suppression of the Prague Spring in 1968 that forced a new strategy on Eurocommunism.

When plans for the invasion of Czechoslovakia became known in Moscow, the secretary general of the Spanish Communist party, Santiago Carrillo, appealed personally to Chairman Brezhnev. He also expressed opposition to the chief party ideologist, Makhail Suslov. The latter's reply summed up the Soviet attitude: the Spanish party has little weight. It represents only a tiny group. Indeed, in 1968 there probably were only some 9,000 party members in Spain and another 15,000 living abroad. Nonetheless, after the invasion the independent Spanish radio transmitter condemned the Russian action, defying Moscow. Asked in retrospect whether Czechoslovakian socialism was in danger, chief Spanish ideologist Manuel Azcarate replied: "To answer 'yes' is not only to make the truth ludicrous, but to deride socialism."[17]

Carrillo has been attacked overtly by the Russian press. The magazine *Party Line*, for example, spoke out as early as 1974: "He sits side by side with declared enemies of the Soviet socialist system."[18] Having lived through the Spanish civil war and spent long years fighting Franco's dictatorship, Carrillo insists he will have nothing to do with a Communist pope, dogma, or excommunication from the Kremlin.

Before he was eighteen, Carrillo had already been arrested twice and jailed for his work as secretary general of socialist youth. General Franco once described him as the most dangerous because he has recognized that all Spaniards are patriots. In 1970, Moscow tried unsuccessfully to unseat Carrillo as Spanish party leader. His book *Eurocommunism and the State* repeats and expands his criticism of Moscow. He has now concluded that a representative democracy joined with worker representation can bring a socialist system to Spain. Whether they agree or not, other Eurocommunist leaders cannot attack Carrillo directly and keep a popular following. However, their support has been ambiguous.

Will Eurocommunists really protect human rights if they come to power? At the same time that they claim to oppose totalitarianism, they continue fraternal contacts with Russia. Former Secretary of State Kissinger has expressed strong misgivings.[19] No Communist party, having come to power, has surrendered that power in a democratic election. The issue of principle concerns the individual's relation to the state, indeed his dignity and worth. In practice, Eurocommunists cannot ignore completely the fact that half a million persons who formerly held party cards in Czechoslovakia continue to be disenfranchised. Many of the leaders, now without human rights, had contact with Western European Communists before the Prague Spring. In late January of 1977, Georges Marchais, head of the French Communist party, explained at a press conference, "What is going on in Czechoslovakia goes against our ideal. The mechanisms which exist in socialist lands should be used to enable men to participate in the building and completion of a socialist society. This is not possible without discussion and conflict of ideas. One must allow the debate which makes possible progress. One cannot make a people happy against its will."[20]

Following a television discussion with a Czechoslovakian Communist in exile, the chief editor of the French Communist newspaper, *Humanité,* wrote: "It is good to see the reality even when it is bitter. There are still threats to freedom. We have shown that we are against them. We will do it again when necessary."[21]

Italy

Italy has the largest Western European Communist party, and the greatest election gains have been made in that country. After World War II, the Communists won 19 percent of the votes; in 1972, 28 percent; in 1975, 32 percent; and in 1976, 35 percent.[22] The Italian Communist party has a long history; it shared in the struggle against Mussolini's fascism. Its most important postwar thinker was Antonio Gramsci. While in fascist imprisonment, he surmised that the Communists could not come to power simply from support by urban workers; they needed the broader base which has now been established. Accepting parliamentary democracy, he spoke of the predominance of the workers more than the dictatorship of the proletariat. Italian Communist theoreticians approached the success of European integration with more objectivity than their counterparts in other countries.

They did not dismiss it simply with charges of monopoly, much less of American imperialism. Indeed, they concluded that much of the strength of the Italian Christian Democrats came from their larger European contacts.

Italian Communists recognize that a totalitarian system would not be accepted in Western Europe today, and they disavow it in their party platform. After Khrushchev's speech denouncing Stalin, Italian Communist leaders spoke of polycentrism. The Prague Spring confirmed their view. At the Communist conference of parties in June, 1969, the Italian delegation rejected the domination of any single party while still accepting Communist internationalism. In October, 1973, party leader Enrico Berlinguer again proposed a compromise between Communists and Christian Democrats. Subsequently, he has argued that Marxism is not an "ideological creed" but an analytical method, and that his party is "lay and democratic, and as such not theist, atheist, or anti-theist."

The present Italian Communist party platform explicitly denies that Marxism-Leninism is a static body of principles which stands above history and must always be applied in the same way. Private property is recognized and the law of the market is accepted as an economic reality. Party strategy is to avoid unnecessary antireligious arguments and anti-clericalism. Artistic freedom of expression is advocated in contradiction to Russian policy.

Unita, the Italian Communist newspaper, observed at the end of 1976, "In the last years, the appearance of divergent political and ideological means can be observed in socialist countries which justify some universal judgments."[23] The paper noted that the problem presented by dissidents is a real one, involving personal rights and the exchange of opinions. "Here is the essence of the question: the state not only claims exclusive political leadership, but also takes direct control over the entire community rights. Intellectuals are isolated and culture restricted."[24] *Unita* calls for critical judgment in the building of a real socialism, not a monolith.

The Turin Communist newspaper concluded that Eurocommunism has become more than just a regional variant. "The truth is that there is a cleft between two general perspectives. It concerns the question of the relationship between socialism and freedom."[25] Clearly, Italian Communism has gained strength by advocating East-West détente, peace, coexistence, and freedom.

Critics point out that the Italian Communist party remains authoritarian in its internal structure, practicing "democratic centralism." How much the platform, now official ideology, has reached into lower party ranks is not clear. Whatever power the Italian Communists acquire in government must be checked by that of other parties if democracy is to be preserved. There are many unanswered questions. What will happen to NATO if the Communists enter the government? Lenin continues to be praised as a tactician. But the fact remains that Eurocommunists are making statements on human rights. Whether they will be honored remains to be seen. Even if President Carter kept silent—as Moscow wishes—they still would be speaking out, at least to the extent of their own self-interest.

East German Protest

Robert Havemann has been described as the only Eurocommunist in Eastern Europe. A member of the Communist party since 1932, a resistance fighter against the Nazis, he is the leading East German dissident. He is a physicist, somewhat the counterpart of Sakharov. Havemann, however, remains a convinced Communist. He argues that Marxism is a science, but not a natural science. Mistakenly, he alleges, it has become an ideology.

"The original wealth of ideas has rigidified into lifeless dogma and doctrines which, with blinkered narrowmindedness, endeavor to force the infinite variety of life and nature onto their Procrustean bed."[26] Havemann finds that Communist dogmatists are isolated, aloof from the world, and sectarian. He wishes to remain open to new ideas. "We want to examine all views and, whenever possible, extract from all ideas and opinions whatever correct and valuable features they may contain, and make them our property."[27]

The sole threat to socialism, Havemann maintains, is the form of the state now predominant in East Germany. Corruption, terror, persecution, and repression are rampant. At the same time, privileged persons in East Germany live better than the rich in the West. Why has no U.N. commission come to investigate, Havemann asks. He claims that the state profits enormously from each product, while wages are low. The Communist system has become the basis for exploitation. He concludes that its economic structure is one of slavery.

Communist professors have invited Havemann to lecture in Italian universities. At home, he is censored and restricted. In effect, an answer to his charges was given by Professor Hermann Kellner of the Institute for Philosophy and Economy, a member of the East German Commission on Human Rights.[28] He emphasizes that human rights have their basis neither in the conscience of the individual nor in religious belief. They can be grounded only in the material class interests of the proletariat. The isolated individual need not be recognized or honored more than society, argues Kellner. For Marxism, production and freedom go together. Thought through to their economic roots, Kellner alleges, human rights require communism. They are not universal privileges; they are class privileges.

Havemann insists that "any restriction or limitation of information or the exchange of information impedes the work of the members of society and hence also the development of social relationships."[29] When people are subjected to mass-produced and officially authorized views, they turn to purely mechanical and superficial thinking. Authorities who fear the consequences of unrestricted information are creating conditions for a disastrous development. "This proves the truth of an ancient thesis of Greek tragedy that man draws upon himself his fate by attempting to avert it."[30]

Rudolf Bahro's book, *The Alternative*, was published in mid-summer of 1977.[31] It is of special importance because it comes from a high-ranking East German economist who has risked not only dismissal but police action by speaking out. Bahro says bluntly that the Communist bureaucracy, bent on its own self-aggrandizement, is out of touch with reality. Practically, there need be no illusion: the pace of work and work morale is not comparable with that in the West. The notion of making a new man is utopian.

Bahro compares the situation to a state religious establishment or theocracy. At least in the case of Christianity, there has been an early model which serves for judgment and renewal. East German communism lacks such reference. Bahro calls for a new democratic party, even if it be a Communist one, as the only possible political solution. He concludes that the Marxist dream of ending alienation with the disappearance of the dominance of man over man has not been realized. Instead, the party bureaucracy, lacking any built-in checks and balances, perpetuates itself inefficiently through class privileges.

Party officials in Eastern Europe have been at pains to avoid all dialogue with Christianity. Communists are to be orthodox Marxists and are compelled to follow the official line. Christians, when identified, are denied all influence or public office. Christianity, although often abused in the past, has the possibility for reform which communism does not. The crisis of human rights will remain in the area as long as the USSR exercises totalitarian control. To close one's eyes to what is going on in the name of peace or détente does no service to victims of tyranny.

6

Black and White: Human Rights in Africa

Today Africa is a center of struggle between the great powers. The crisis of human rights there arises in part from the fact that in the past colonialism was discriminatory and repressive. Native cultures were disregarded and abused. Now indigenous traditions and histories are being recovered amid the search for national identity. Even though independence has arrived throughout most of the continent, economic underdevelopment as well as tribalism complicate the problems of the new nations.

A basic factor in understanding Africa is tribalism. In the past tribalism brought a certain stability, wisdom, and even justice, in spite of the fact that it was accompanied by war and slavery. Today, tribalism has become a source of tension, and at times inhibits the quest for national unity.

Basic rights are often ignored in the search for modernization, economic development, and stability. Western European and American models are not easily understood. A single party often led in the struggle for independence; two-party systems generally have not been adopted. At the same time, the Communist attack on religion seems irrelevant and has not been successful. What will provide conviction strong enough to counter injustice, discrimination, and hatred? In practice, all citizens—black and white alike—

need enough political power to defend themselves against oppressors.

The Children

The scene is downtown Johannesburg, South Africa, during the summer of 1977. Black students line up before the police station.[1] Girls kneel in front and behind them stand the young men. Freedom songs ring out. Black power salutes are given with raised, clenched fists. The "Children" demand the release of twenty of their fellow black students who have been arrested and held by the police. The police resort to violence, leaving many black youths bleeding and reportedly arrested.

The Children are from Soweto, a huge amalgam of segregated black townships on the outskirts of Johannesburg with a population of approximately 1.2 million blacks. Largely high-school students, the Children have assumed political power in Soweto. Their tactics are a mixture of argument, threat, and compulsion. Most of all they demand action. Soweto schoolrooms have been taken over and used for strategy sessions. Orders are issued to all members of the community, including parents. When necessary, opponents have been beaten and bombed.

The Children have been attacked and arrested by police; some have been killed. On the first anniversary of the riots that began on June 16, 1976 and eventually cost more than six hundred lives, the Children ordered a two-day general strike. Hymns of liberation like *Senzenina* ("What Have We Done?") were sung in church services as clenched fists were raised. Community life came to a standstill. Even the four hundred illegal drinking establishments in Soweto were closed. It is reported that some 1,500 "Children" have left for guerilla training outside South Africa.

Gatsha Buthelezi, chief minister of KwaZulu and leader of the Inkatha movement, explains:

Political treachery stalks the land, treachery by the government, secret police, bribery, manipulation, detention without trial. Bannings of people and bannings of organizations are political treachery as far as the majority of South Africans are concerned.[2]

The South African contradiction between an irrational racial policy and a rationally organized, expanding industrial society is blatant. A land in which hundreds of blacks are arrested daily for pass violations claims anticommunism as its defense of apartheid. It is clear that change will not come simply from economic factors. International political pressure is necessary. Deracialization depends on how much the white oligarchy is forced to give in.

Americans fought a war for their independence. They fought a civil war to maintain their unity despite the diverse social and cultural origins of Americans. The poor and oppressed people of the world, therefore, expect Americans to understand and support the struggle of other people to be free and united, even if freedom and unity cannot be won peacefully.[3]

So remarked President Julius K. Nyerere of Tanzania.

Policy

Goler T. Butcher, a former counsel to the House Foreign Affairs subcommittee on Africa, describes the situation in terms of three questions: Will the United States implement policies showing commitment to the principles of the Declaration of Independence? Will the United States realize the meaning of independence, namely, that it must function in a partner relationship with the developing world? Will America comprehend the dynamics of Africa?[4]

"Regrettably," Butcher explains, "*human rights* has become a code term among policy makers for long-term interests which translate into interests that need *not* concern us *now*."[5]

He insists human rights is as much a part of immediate United States interests as economics. Butcher believes the daily violence by which South African whites continue their control and subjugation makes clear the acute danger of the situation. The time for peaceful progress is past.

What is now going on is not just a civil rights struggle but a liberation movement. Butcher believes the only real option is to work for the least possible violence. The United States must make a decision and convey that decision to South Africa: That its policies of racial discrimination and exclusion of the majority from the political process are a threat to world peace. The first step is the message; the second is its implementation.

The particulars of the South African situation ought not to be overlooked. A government is generally regarded as totalitarian when it refuses political opposition and bans advocates of change, free press, and assembly.[6] Characteristically, totalitarian regimes attempt to destroy traditional social groups and replace natural communities with new units sponsored by the state. The South African regime, by contrast, seeks to preserve traditional groups and ideologies, using them to divide and conquer. Of course, it has been concerned to keep urban blacks from becoming politicized. On white-owned farms and in the reserves, widespread illiteracy is still reported, and some blacks speak only their own native languages.

In principle, South Africa seeks to continue the status quo of a hierarchically ordered racial society. The paradox of the situation is that the government has come to power after open elections among whites; vocal opposition has been allowed in Parliament. There is no single dictatorial leader. Apartheid was legally established following the 1948 election victory of the National Party under the "Herrenvolk-democracy" of the dominant white group. Egalitarian aspects of the frontier-settler past are continued. The police use violence but not totalitarian mass terror. Repression is confined to actual opponents of the regime.

Afrikaner History

Whites have been in South Africa for more than three centuries.[7] Native blacks were not present in large numbers at the Cape of Good Hope when Jan van Riebeek first established a refreshment station for ships of the Dutch East India Company in 1652. By the end of the next century, Dutch colonists had developed patterns of language and customs distinguishable from those in their former homeland of Holland. Competition with the English nurtured Afrikaner nationalism. During the Napoleonic wars, the colony was taken over by the British crown, beginning in 1795. In 1820, 5,000 British settlers landed.

In 1836, the Boers who wanted to hold slaves made their Great Trek to found the Independent Republic of Natal. When they had pushed further over the Drakensberg mountains into Transvaal, they subdued Zulu tribesmen at the cost of their own lives in the battle of "Blood River" in 1838. The English made war against the Boer republics and made them British colonies in 1902. Afrikaners have not forgotten that their women and children died by the thousands in British camps, even though the territory was granted independence in the Commonwealth in 1910. Reinforced by religion and folk institutions, Afrikaner nationalism became strong enough to take control after World War II. With it came official apartheid.

White Domination

White domination in South Africa is enforced by a complex system of coercive economic and ideological controls, the most overt being the pass system. Persons of mixed racial background have been downgraded. With the blacks, they live under a system of domestic, internal colonialism. Economic modernization has taken place amid drastically retarded political development. The situation is potentially more explosive and the magnitude of the revolution potentially greater than in other colonial areas because of South Africa's technological development.[8]

White racial domination is overtly evident as direct political exploitation. Police and the law courts are used publicly in the enforcement of apartheid, since race has been made the criterion for citizenship. The oligarchy has made it an effective means of domination. Sociologically, South Africa is both metropolis and colony. The white settlers cannot just move out and grant full independence to their subjects. They have no homeland to which to return.

South Africa has had a larger number of black university graduates and earlier detribalization and urbanization than most other areas of the continent. The black part of the population can be divided about a third each among the urban proletariat, farm workers, and those living in native reserves. Nine politically independent states are planned for the very limited part of the land where blacks are to be provided independence and full citizenship. The solution is unacceptable and unfair to the blacks. U.N. Ambassador Andrew Young has emphasized that the problem is racism, not communism. As another observer noted, "Nobody needs to read Marx to react with hostility to brutality."[9]

Change?

Prior to the Carter administration, U.S. policy in Southern Africa followed a classic cold-war strategy.[10] Its goals were regional stability, continuance in power of anti-Communist governments, and maintenance of an area for increasing corporate investments.

South Africa is the most highly industrialized part of the

continent. Its industrial revolution was sparked by the discovery of diamonds at Kimberley in 1869. In addition to unusual mineral resources, there is also an abundance of relatively cheap labor. Transportation, communication, and water supplies have been developed carefully. The area was largely agricultural until the end of World War II. Subsequently, major investment capital has flowed into the country. At the same time, civil liberties have been withheld from the black population.

American Policy

The issue is clear: It is futile to advocate human rights throughout the rest of the continent when apartheid is left unchallenged.

During his election campaign, Jimmy Carter argued:

Africa needs development assistance and technological advances which only the United States can supply, and the United States needs both the resources and markets of an emerging Africa.

* * *

It is in the interest of the United States to avoid further bloodshed in southern Africa. It is also in the interest of black Africa to settle the question of African liberation without violence. The oppression of apartheid is a systematic policy of institutional violence under law by the South African government, while the oppression in certain black-ruled states of Africa is the result of a particular dictator and the attempt to deal with historic tribal tension or the vestiges of colonially inspired division. . . . We must condemn injustice wherever it is and whatever the color of its originators.[11]

The *Wall Street Journal*, in a commentary entitled "Getting Serious," noted that President Carter draws an analogy between South Africa and the civil rights struggle in the South of his own country.[12] In the United States, clear moral imperatives could be discerned. However, these are not as evident in Africa. The issue is not simply one of black majority rule; its realization does not insure justice.

The *Wall Street Journal* writer pointed out that the civil rights movement in the United States invoked equal opportunity and due process. It was not simply a drive for majority rule. In the end, however, the American society's essential liberalism supported the movement. By contrast, the commentary found little prospect for liberal-style due process for Africans today. Black majority rule too often has allowed human rights to become moribund.

Military Dictators

Less than two months after his inauguration, President Carter remarked at a press conference that the murders in Uganda had "disgusted the entire civilized world."[13] He supported the British demand that an investigation "go into Uganda to assess the horrible murders that apparently are taking place in that country—the persecution of those who have aroused the ire of Mr. Amin." Carter himself aroused Amin's ire and the dictator sent his soldiers to round up Americans living in the country and deliver them to the capital, together with their "chickens, goats, pigs, and any other animals." He also forbade them to leave Uganda.

The Ugandian Chargé d'Affairs in Washington assured the state department that Amin "merely wants to meet the people to reassure them that nothing will happen to them." Not so for his own subjects. It is said that he seeks to annihilate the two tribes that formed the power base for his predecessor, Milton Obote—the Acholi and Lango tribes. At Mugire prison, truckloads of troops from these tribes were reportedly strangled. Only a few African leaders such as Tanzania's Julius Nyerere and Zambia's Kenneth Kaunda have spoken out in protest.

Nearly half of Africa is under the rule of military or military-civilian coalitions.[14] The development of military regimes has not been limited to countries with inherently inviable economies, deep ethnic cleavages, or those lacking preparation for self-government. Nor is army rule necessarily more efficient, less corrupt, or less tribally oriented than that of civilians. The military dictator has sometimes been imagined as progressive, as working for transformation of society rather than as incompetent, corrupt, and reactionary. The facts prove otherwise. Army and police acquire an overbearing importance in such situations due to the weakness of national institutions. The dominance of the military does not insure economic development; greed continues. The Ugandan army is probably more corrupt than the regime before Amin.

Amin

One-party rule can be illustrated by the case of Amin's rule in Uganda.[15] The dictator is a product of the harsh, backward, and isolated environment of the West Nile periphery. Gregarious and ruthless, he appeals to the naiveté of the common man. A Moslem in a land with a Christian majority, he fought for the British, with whom he seems to have a love-hate relationship. At first, the general pledged interim military rule. Now, victims of his massacres number tens, probably hundreds, of thousands.

The country where Amin seized power in January of 1971 is made up of twenty-one major ethnic groups. There are more than thirty tribes, eighteen numbering more than 100,000. British colonial rule favored the largest tribe, the Baganda. Its members, Westernized from the top on down, became a source of trained personnel. The British situated their capital in Baganda territory. Their rule was accepted in a voluntary agreement which gave the king, the *Kabaka,* co-equal status with the colonial power. After independence, tribalism worked against national unity. When Kaba Mutesa II appealed for foreign intervention, his home at Mmengo Hill was attacked. Disguised as a commoner, he fled into exile.

Although the country was 49 percent Roman Catholic, 28 percent Protestant, and 5.5 percent Moslem, the British favored Protestantism. Roman Catholic-Protestant competition as well as civilian-military tension worked against democracy. It has been said that it was not nationalist agitation that led to Uganda's independence. Rather, the imminence of independence gave birth to nationalist parties. Ugandan political parties have been traditionally decentralized, parochial, regional, and personal. Trying to develop central **rule** in a united state, Amin's predecessor, Obote, abolished press freedom and opposition parties and instituted preventive detention. The army, which at the time of independence had numbered only about a thousand soldiers, was expanded manyfold.

Factionalism, ethnic cleavages, and intercommand jealousies ruled in the military. Amin feared being displaced. Since his coup he has manipulated the army, purged various camps, and brought in new recruits. Economics has suffered with the decline of human rights. Uganda has a limited variety of crops; cotton is the most important. The Asian community that controlled trade and first welcomed Amin was expelled dramatically.

Abuse of Human Rights

Keba M'baya, president of the Supreme Court of Senegal, spoke at the twenty-ninth session of the Commission of the Rights of Man at the United Nations, Geneva.[16] The jurist pointed to serious violations of human rights in Africa: slavery, forced labor, denial of freedom of association, and detention without trial. Too often, he explained, separation of the branches of government has been abandoned in favor of extraordinary powers. Human rights requires respect for the rule of law and a disinterested judiciary. Unfortunately, controversy is often regarded not as a matter to be resolved by objective adjudication but as a personal challenge which must be overcome. A citizen protesting a violation of his rights seems to be attacking personally the official involved. Such attitudes need to be evaluated against the background of African history.

Earlier, society was organized tribally under powerful rulers. Kings were believed to be divinely ordained. Nonetheless, there were checks and balances on power. Major decisions were not made without some form of prior consultation, generally with the elders of the tribe. Relatively small and simple societies had a certain social equilibrium and stability.

The introduction of firearms and subsequent colonization changed all this. Nationalism has replaced colonialism. With it has come one-party rule in most countries. Some observers regard such a policy as the only way to mobilize the masses. Others view it as an instrument of dictatorship. Dictators such as Amin have attempted to destroy all opposition. Dissent is generally labeled subversive. Elections have disappeared in many countries. In others they are mere formalities. In certain places, one-party rule has contributed to economic and social development. TANU in Tanzania and UNITA in Zambia seem to function in this way. In principle, however, economic progress is no substitute for human rights—free speech, free press, and freedom of assembly. Amin, in fact, came to power because of the failure of popular democracy.

A high illiteracy rate and poverty work against human rights in many African countries. Education and a fair standard of living are necessary for freedom. By itself, due process of law is not enough. The struggle between the politically powerful and the powerless becomes more brutal when no universal principles are recognized. Security forces with unlimited power are a threat to citizens. The will of a dictator takes the place of both the executive and judiciary. Every member of the secret police is a mobile court.

Contrary to the actions of General Amin, the Koran teaches about the relationship of piety to justice. Moreover, the Christian conviction is that all human beings are equal before God. The God of the Bible is not just an abstraction outside of human history. He stands for peace, justice, and love, and He calls men to work for these ends. Righteous, just, and loving, He cares about the poor and oppressed. Today, Christian churches often find themselves out of favor with authoritarian regimes—black and white.

Trials

The cause of human rights in Africa may be summarized by looking at a number of trials:

In his book *La Grande Mystification du Congo-Kisnishasa,* Cléophas Kamitatu, former minister of foreign affairs, cites the minutes of a trial in Zaire in which an earlier prime minister and some of his colleagues were sentenced to death for conspiracy.[17] When it became clear that no evidence to support the charge would be produced by the prosecution, one of the defendants began to shout questions: "Did I threaten to kill the commander-in-chief of the army with the rifles I had at home? Did we possess arms? Did we organize a gang to go and kill the President? . . . I ask you those questions and I ask you to pass judgment justly." The head of the court acknowledged that he was under orders from the executive by saying, "Gentlemen, this is a court-martial. We are not here to discuss; we are here to punish someone."

The month after President Carter was inaugurated, General Amin convened a giant rally at Kampala, the capital.[18] The state ministers in charge of internal affairs and of land and water attended, together with the Most Reverend Janani Luwum, Anglican Archbishop of Uganda. At the rally, some lesser suspects read confessions implicating the three men. When they were charged with being agents of the exiled Milton Obote, the Archbishop smiled and shook his head in disbelief. Amin's soldiers cried out, "Kill them all." The dictator insisted there would be a proper military trial. The following day, Radio Uganda reported that all three of the accused men had been killed in an automobile accident. The car transporting them to an interrogation center collided with another vehicle and overturned as they attempted to overpower the driver and escape. Churchmen disbelieved the report.

Two trials took place in Pretoria, the administrative capital of South Africa, in mid-summer of 1977. They were held before red-robed judges addressed as "Your Lordship" by black-robed lawyers.[19] The first was the trial of Breyton Breytenbach, 37, a white Afrikaner poet. Originally, Breytenbach had been charged with being a revolutionary. An organizational chart, weapons, and manuals had been produced before his first sentencing in 1975. Now they were disregarded as largely figments of his imagination. International pressure resulted in his acquittal.

Two blocks from the white man's trial, the government charged twelve blacks with terrorism. All were members of the outlawed African National Congress. Each day at noon they raised their hands in the black power salute and were answered by the clenched fists of black spectators in the courtroom. For four days the state's leading witness, Ian Deway Rwaxa, explained how the defendants were linked to the Soviet Union and China. Then he recanted and denied the truth of all that he had said against his fellow blacks. He said he had been beaten daily, strangled, suffocated, kept naked in a cold cell by the police, and forced to lie. At the end of three months of solitary confinement, he had been taken to see his son. The police had placed money in his hand to give to the child, making the father understand he would never see him again unless he cooperated.

After he changed his testimony, Rwaxa could be charged with perjury. When one of the lawyers in the case was asked privately if this would be done, he replied, "No, I don't think he will be charged. I don't think he'll ever see a courtroom again. I don't think that we will ever see him alive." The lawyer added that it took enormous courage to do what the witness had done. In spite of Rwaxa's admission, the defendants were convicted.

Racialism makes mockery of European and American appeals for human rights. The tragedy of the situation is that white South Africans picture themselves as defenders of Western civilization and Christianity. Religious practice is widespread. Indeed, attempts are still made to justify racial discrimination on biblical grounds.

At the same time that tension mounts, South Africa apparently has the capacity to produce and use nuclear weapons.

7

Terrorism — Disarmament — Hunger

The following incident has been envisaged in a variety of forms: Five or ten years from now, a hundred kilograms of plutonium are hijacked while en route from one country to another. The police keep the theft a secret as long as possible. Authorities do not wish to alarm the public. Finally, the head of state receives a letter stating that an underground organization will explode a nuclear weapon in the next few days. The press and radio receive copies of the letter. The explosion occurs in a remote wilderness area. The head of state appears on television, urging the public to keep calm. No person has been killed by the blast.

A subsequent letter—sent to the chief executive, newspapers, and television—reports that nuclear weapons have been hidden in three large cities. These will be exploded if specific demands are not met. What should a government do? Should it ignore the notes? Can it afford to be under the command of a small, unknown terrorist group?

Nuclear terrorism could be one of the most important moral problems of the next fifty years. Methods for building nuclear bombs are public knowledge; models have been constructed by college students. Such bombs could be built and used by international gangsters or irresponsible nations!

Today, only a limited number of countries are known to have nuclear weapons: the United States, Russia, Great

Britain, France, China, and India. There are rumors others from South Africa to Korea are developing such weapons. By 1985, forty countries will have nuclear power plants; by 1995, one hundred. George Rathjens, an MIT expert, calculated that by the end of the century there will be one thousand nuclear reactors capable of producing 50,000 bombs.[1]

Technology

Today, a country wishing to have nuclear weapons still has to undertake an expensive program of development. But this is changing. The power to build bombs comes with the keys to a reactor. A country need not decide it wants to accumulate stocks for nuclear weapons. They are at hand! A standard reactor can produce as much as two hundred kilograms of plutonium per year; a crude bomb requires only ten kilograms.[2] Control of nuclear wastes, from which enriched plutonium is made, has become of utmost urgency. While still a candidate, Carter called attention to the problem, and President Ford tightened regulations. Although U.S. policy has become more careful, the acute danger of the situation has not disappeared.

The illusion that there are two atoms—one for peace and one for war—has been shattered. This simply is not the case. Part of the present danger could have been avoided by a more careful policy. The U.S. Atoms for Peace program uses a spin-off from the World War II atomic projects, the so-called light-water reactor. A different type of reactor could have been developed. Fred Ikle, former Director of the Arms Control and Disarmament Agency, explains: "We could have chosen a course that might have greatly reduced the risks of nuclear proliferation without any loss in terms of economical operation of power reactors."[3]

Present U.S. policy attempts to minimize the danger by controlling the distribution of enriched plutonium. Uranium, as mined, has only a 0.7 percent concentration of the isotope U-235. Not readily suited for nuclear reactors, it must be enriched to about 3 percent. If such enrichment were the only way material for a bomb could be made available, the situation would be less difficult. However, much cheaper nuclear fuel can be obtained at the back end of the process. After the enriched uranium has been consumed, plutonium can be made from waste through chemical separation at relatively small cost. Clearly, not just the initial fuel but also its end product requires monitoring. The International Atomic Energy Agency, with headquarters in Vienna, attempts regulation but lacks effective power.

The problem is not primarily an American-Russian one. A Soviet arms control expert remarked, "Our interests on proliferation are almost identical with you Americans."[4] The issue is worldwide. William Anders, former chairman of the Nuclear Regulatory Commission, argues, "The only way to have our way is to be involved, not to opt out, to set the pace, to set the moral tone, if you will."[5]

On June 27, 1975, West Germany concluded an agreement with Brazil, promising to sell a whole nuclear industry to the South American country for eight billion dollars. American companies had sought to do business with Brazil, but the U.S. government refused approval because the proposed deal included techniques for uranium enrichment and chemical separation. West Germans defend their treaty by arguing that American firms have about 70 percent of the market for reactors; German industry is entitled to its fair share. Their position only complicates problems of disarmament. The fact that neither West Germany nor Brazil were known to have nuclear weapons at the time of their agreement does not preclude their "overnight" manufacture in time of need.

Disarmament

An MIT arms control expert has pointed out that the world has grown used to having the equivalent of fifteen tons of TNT under every bed just the way men formerly accepted the fact that the plague would strike. Any responsible person who does not remain permanently alarmed about the present arms race, he concludes, has lost touch with reality. To date, détente has not brought about disarmament.

Immediately after President Carter's remarks on human rights at a town meeting in Clinton, Massachusetts, he spoke about disarmament:

> I want our country to be the focal point for deep concern about human beings all over the world. I am trying to search with the Soviet Union for a way to reduce the horrible arms race, where we've spent billions and billions and billions of dollars on atomic weapons. We are no more secure now than we were 8 years ago or 12 years ago or 16 years ago. We're much more deeply threatened by more and more advanced weapons. So, we are dealing with the Soviet Union, quietly and diplomatically, and, I hope effectively, to search out a way to reduce dependence on weapons without damaging at all our nation's own security.[6]

A moral foreign policy—one which is non-suicidal—must have immediate and long-range objectives. There is a double responsibility: not only the reversal of the strategic arms race but the maintenance of deterrence.

For the present, deterrence is imperative. The United States must be armed in such a way that no surprise first strike can possibly succeed in wiping out its retaliatory capacity. The long-range intention is the reversal of the strategic arms race. In his inaugural address Carter announced his ultimate goal to be the elimination of all nuclear weapons from this earth. Is this possible without compromise of human rights? Carter argues that the risk of nuclear war cannot be tolerated indefinitely.

A U.S. Department of Defense analysis, made as long ago

as Secretary McNamara's tenure, is still cited as valid today.[7] Researchers concluded that four hundred deliverable strategic warheads would inflict intolerable damage on Russia. Thirty percent of the people and three-fourths of the Russian industrial capacity would be destroyed in such an attack. A single Poseidon-firing submarine can launch enough nuclear warheads to do as much as one-third of the entire destruction.

It is of first importance to recognize that unlimited weapons are not necessary to national survival. The prime absurdity of the nuclear arms race is that in order to deter, one need not have real weapons, but rather the belief on the part of another that one has such weapons.[8] If the secret could be kept, plywood or plastic missiles would do the deterrent job and save a fortune. Thousands of suicidal weapons have been stockpiled for decades. Future historians may speak retrospectively of a world gone mad.

In his *Anatomy of Human Destructiveness*, psychologist Erich Fromm observes that a good deal of paranoid thinking is to be found in foreign policy. It is assumed that "what is possible must be considered to be a basis for decisions, rather than what is probable." The nuclear arms race brings impoverishment: "Politically it restricts freedom; psychologically it creates fear and apathy." Fromm concludes, "In our obsession to consider all possibilities, we end up by not considering the real possibilities."[9]

Russia

Addressing the U.N. General Assembly, President Carter said:

> The Soviet Union and the United States have accumulated thousands of nuclear weapons. Our two nations now have five times more missile warheads today than we had just eight years ago. But we are not five times more secure. On the contrary,

the arms race has only increased the risk of conflict. . . . The arms race is now embedded in the very fabric of international affairs and can only be contained with the greatest difficulty. . . . the security of both countries and the entire world is threatened.

. . . My preference would be for strict controls or even a freeze on new types and new generations of weaponry with a deep reduction in the strategic arms of both sides. Such a major step towards not only arms limitation but arms reduction would be welcomed by mankind as a giant step toward peace.[10]

Fred Ikle urges, "It is important that we do not allow the Russians to stifle our ambitions for genuine disarmament. President Carter deserves strong support for reaching forward to achieve substantial and balanced arms reduction."[11]

Russian tactics seek to influence the West by a combination of force and persuasion. Ikle observes that in the USSR there are no experts or parliamentarians who offer compromises. The malleable amalgam of views held by government officials, news media, and private experts in the United States has no counterpart in Russia.

Linkage

To suppose that Carter's stand on human rights will really deter the Russians from disarmament negotiations when this is in their own self-interest is a position that lacks tough-mindedness. "Competition and rivalry between the two systems in the world arena continues," Brezhnev said in a public address. "The crux of the matter is only to see to it that this process does not develop into armed clashes between the countries. . . ."[12]

Some critics argue that détente has allowed Moscow to conduct a campaign to influence and control key areas of the world while strengthening its economy and armaments by means of Western technology and industrial know-how.

Ikle reports that the Russians have developed seven new intercontinental ballistic missiles since 1972, while the United States has developed only one. The Russians have built up to and exceeded the number of American missiles. Their missiles are much bigger, more substantially modernized, and more numerous than American missiles. If parity is set at lower levels, they will have to make the greater reduction.

The United States counterbalances with the neutron bomb and the cruise missile.[13] The latter is low-flying with a range of more than 1,500 miles. Only twenty feet long and twenty inches in diameter, it can deliver the equivalent of ten Hiroshima bombs to within one hundred feet of its programmed target. The weapon, powered by tiny jet engines, is guided by miniaturized computers. It is not a true missile because it does not follow a ballistic course. The cruise is more similar to the German V-I buzz bombs from World War II. The Russians at present lag behind the United States in this development. It is estimated that it would take them at least five years to catch up.

Paul Warnke, successor to Ikle as chief SALT negotiator and director of the U.S. Arms Control and Disarmament Agency, warns that everyone will be less secure than before if the arms race continues.[14] Technology is destabilizing. There is the perennial danger of new weapons. When one side develops a system not covered by an arms agreement, such as the neutron bomb and the cruise missile, the other side feels compelled to counter it. One cannot expect that the Soviet Union will do anything but pursue its own self-interest. But what is its self-interest?

Arthur Macy Cox, in *The Dynamics of Détente: How to End the Arms Race,* quotes Erich Fromm:

> The only sane mode of thinking in matters of foreign policy is to . . . be aware of the fact that our opponents are as little suicidal as we are and have the same interest in survival and in

the progress of their society; yet paranoid-like thinking is mutually infectious.[15]

Cox argues that the first genuine steps toward disarmament will be the hardest. However, once the progress has started, he believes, it will become dynamic. On any terms, prevention of nuclear war is directly related to the survival of the major powers. Atomic and hydrogen weapons unleashed would make mockery of human rights.

Negotiation

The first SALT agreement was preceded by two years of hard bargaining. If nuclear war is to be avoided, there must be negotiation. Is this to be at the expense of human rights? Unless nations talk at the conference table, they may go to war, destroying one another in a nuclear holocaust. If Western democracies are not to capitulate in the face of totalitarianism, human rights diplomacy must be a part of such negotiation. It was the Western European nations, not the United States, which insisted that human rights guarantees be written into the Helsinki pact. Compliance, it was agreed, would be monitored by a series of conferences that would continue indefinitely into the future.

Subsequently, West Europeans have been concerned that these conferences should not be broken off by propaganda charges and countercharges. Specifically, they do not want to give the Russian delegation an excuse to leave the conference table; instead they want to continue to engage it with its East European allies. Of course, this does not mean that firm and responsible pressure for compliance with human rights provisions should not continue. On the contrary, ongoing discussion is a necessary strategy. Reform, not revolution, is the long-term goal.

The smaller countries of Europe have been a creative center of civilization and culture. Divided after World War

II, the continent's political and military position (exclusive of Russia) is not as strong as before. There should be little surprise that the British, French, and West German delegates wish to avoid a confrontation between the United States and the USSR. They understand that for the possibility of political, economic, social, or religious change and improvement to exist, it is important that lines of communication be kept open. Indeed, the intention of the Helsinki agreement was not to resolve fully all problems of human rights. The hope was rather to facilitate the exchange of ideas and persons.

It is important for the United States to participate in the campaign for human rights. Both isolationism and imperialism are dangerous. The possibility of isolation has been destroyed by science and technology. The country is no longer protected by two oceans, as it was in the nineteenth century. Imperialism not only risks violating human rights, but it also becomes self-defeating. American intervention in Vietnam represented an attempt to solve a political problem by a military strategy. It failed in spite of many good intentions. A more effective policy is to work for greater respect for human rights in all countries. Patience is needed for results.

Solzhenitsyn, in *August 1914*, attempted to appraise the reason for Russia's defeat in World War I.[16] This historical novel is both sympathetic and critical of his fellow countrymen. The Tsarist rulers expected the land mass of their country to defeat the Germans as it had the French at the time of Napoleon. Identifying God with country, they trusted in their own invincibility. The revolutionaries Solzhenitsyn describes in *Lenin in Zurich* did not share this belief.[17] They came to power as Tsarist illusions were shattered by the reality of events. Complacency led to defeat. Solzhenitsyn warns against it most of all in defense of human rights today. He accepts Christianity as the ultimate justification of human rights.

Christianity illumines the complexity of contemporary issues more than other less profound views. The world cannot be divided into black and white issues, into good and evil nations. The fact is that no state, not even the strongest, can live in complete isolation. A half-century after the Russian revolution, respect for human rights is imperative for the survival of civilization.

Classifications of nations distinguish not only a Third and Fourth World of developing nations, some rich and some poor, but also a Fifth World of about thirty acutely poor countries. Human rights will not be secure until there is an end of hunger, illiteracy, and lack of medical care.

Ambassador Andrew Young

It is said that U.N. Ambassador Andrew Young and President Carter think alike on human rights. Brought to office by the President, Young represents an important aspect of administration thinking. In fact, Young helped win a major block of votes for Carter. Addressing the graduates of Michigan State University at commencement in the spring of 1977, Young commented, "By a hair's breadth we have escaped disaster in this country, and we now are on the edge of another crisis—and another opportunity."[18] Young then summed his view of the world situation:

●*A steadily escalating world arms race.* The annual world military budget was $350 billion in 1976. This amount is equal to the annual gross product of the two billion people in the poorer half of the world.

●*Massive social and economic problems* in the world that can finally tend to destabilize the international order.

●*Continued escalation of world hunger and famine* in spite of unusually high harvests in recent years.

●*Global unemployment and underemployment.* The gap between rich and poor, between employed and educated and unemployed and uneducated, is continuing to grow.

• *The world energy crisis* could wreck the economic system of the industrialized nations in twenty years unless massive and serious remedies are started within the next five or ten years.

• *Spread of repressive regimes worldwide*. The question of human rights is fundamental. Young explained: "Only a repressive regime can cope with rising social pressures if there is no development."

Young reminded the graduates of the class of 1977 that the Marshall Plan had been proposed thirty years earlier at a Harvard commencement. He described it as a bold and thoughtful response to a grave situation. Recently liberated European countries were in danger of collapse and possible domination by the ruthless Stalinist government of the Soviet Union. "Like those graduating seniors of 1947, many of us probably are still basking in the close call of escaping—from Vietnam and Watergate in our case, World War II in their case—and thus not fully aware of our great danger."

The ambassador proposed "development" as a creative response to the world situation. "Increasingly we are recognizing that 'development' as applied to societies means about the same thing as it does when applied to people. . . . It means that a person is moving towards realization of his or her full potential as a person." Of course this is impossible without human rights.

Young judges that the problems of 1977 are much more difficult than those of 1947. "The danger of chaos, dictatorship, and economic stagnation is worldwide, or at least as wide as the underdeveloped and developing world, which includes most of the nations of Latin America, Africa, and Asia." Chaos and stagnation can breed tyranny and repression. How can the United States promote human rights?

A legalistic, dogmatic, or defensive approach is impotent. In working for human rights, economic and political development must go hand in hand. It is important to note that Young has consistently advocated cooperation between government and private enterprise. He has argued that large corporations, being innovative and creative, have common interests with governments in underdeveloped countries. At the same time, human rights cannot be effective without a better quality of life. Massive investment in human resources is needed, such as a sharing of skills with the Third World—technical skills, social skills, teaching skills, organizational skills.

Young's argument is that in an era in which nations are so interdependent, a community of interests and values must be built up or the world will destroy itself in chaos. A whole new moral and religious vision is imperative. Idealism has become realism. In such a situation, world politics is the struggle for world development. Tragically, the arms race vitiates and weakens any attempt to meet human problems. "To preserve our scarce world resources, to . . . promote human rights and dignity, to help freedom grow," these are all compelling reasons which make "world development . . . in the interest of every person and every nation." Young concludes from his Christian conviction that the struggle is not simply to change things outside one's own self. It is a struggle to change one's own perceptions and attitudes toward other peoples and nations. "If we can win the struggle with ourselves," he says, "the rest of the battles will be easy."

8
Military Rule in Latin America

Mauricio Lopez had served as rector of the National University at San Luis, Argentina. Recently he had accepted an appointment as a professor of philosophy in the Institute of Theological Studies in Buenos Aires. An internationally known Protestant Christian, he was dedicated, intelligent, and responsible. His disappearance is part of a reign of terror that has decimated university faculties. In the early hours of the new year, 1977, he was kidnaped from his home by eight hooded men. He has not been seen or heard from again and is presumed dead. His case is only one of many.[1]

Military dictatorships control a large part of South America. Their leaders argue that the suppression of terrorism is the most urgent problem in their countries. The maintenance of public order is not just an academic issue in these lands, but the question remains as to whether it can be fairly used to justify police-sanctioned strategies. The wave of violence encouraged by Cuba has now declined. Meanwhile, police repression continues uncontrolled even as the contrast between rich and poor remains desperate under military rule. Large masses of humanity, urban and rural, live in poverty; their human rights—social and political—languish.

Dictatorship

The United States has claimed a sphere of influence in Latin America since the Monroe Doctrine 150 years ago. Does concern for human rights needlessly endanger North American influence by interference in the internal affairs of friendly states? On the contrary, it may free it from identification with reactionary regimes.

To be sure, foreign policy issues are not simple. Strong feelings of hostility, as well as admiration and respect, for the United States are longstanding among Latin Americans. Unfortunately, in the past Washington has too often been identified with dictators in the popular mind. Most Latin American republics have human rights guarantees on their statute books and no country except Cuba has officially renounced a traditional democratic model for a Marxist one. But rights that are granted on paper are not necessarily realities. Today, arbitrary arrest, torture, and terrorist murder are widespread.

Guerilla Terror

In September of 1968, Carlos Marighela, the Che Guevara of Brazil, proclaimed that guerillas under his leadership would let "loose both in the cities and in the countryside such a large number of armed incidents that the government will be compelled to change the political situation of the country into a military situation."[2] Such a strategy was "to displease the masses, who will then rise against the police and the government soldiers whom they consider to be responsible for this state of affairs."[3] In the manual of the urban guerilla, Marighela wrote:

> The government will be compelled to intensify repression and this will make life intolerable for the citizens. Homes will be broken into, police raids will be organized, innocent people

arrested and channels of communication shut down. Police terror will be set up and more and more political assassinations will take place; there will be massive political persecution.[4]

Such documents evoked only limited support. In a survey in Rio de Janeiro in July, 1969, 79 percent of the populace condemned terrorism.[5] For a decade, leftist guerilla activity has been answered increasingly by government-sanctioned violence.

Communism in Cuba encouraged terror throughout Latin America. Lack of education and health care, along with minimal living conditions, seemed to predispose revolution. On his own island, Castro had overthrown an inefficient dictator whom the United States no longer supported with arms. It soon became evident, however, that something other than the Communist pattern is necessary amid poverty and underdevelopment. What began as a political revolution in the end destroyed most of the Cuban middle class. Cuba has become a client of the USSR rather than the United States. Drastic social improvement is still needed throughout Latin America—but with respect for human rights.

It must be recognized that political takeover by the military often brings not the alleviation of difficulties, but the continuation of violence. A widespread pattern of arbitrary arrest, suppression of information, torture, kidnaping, and murder is evident. Military regimes lack popular support in spite of occasional elections. The decline of older economic and political elites under pressures of modernization and industrialization has left a vacuum of instability and division between left and right. There is, of course, no utopian solution for complex political issues.

Authoritarian traditions are longstanding.[6] Monarchy continued in Brazil throughout most of the last century. Spanish and Portuguese colonial rule was oligarchic and royalist rather than popular democratic. The native population was controlled by a small minority of nobility and clergy who claimed culture and privilege. The movement for independence began at the time of Napoleon and came partly in response to European political developments.

Chile

Argentina and Brazil have had only brief periods of free democratic rule. Chile, by contrast, had a remarkably stable multi-party democracy until 1973.[7] In many respects the demise of human rights was most tragic in that country. Elsewhere constitutions had been made and remade. Chile had had only two such documents since 1833. Under the Christian Democrats, before Allende, 51 percent of the ownership of the large copper concerns was already in government hands; agrarian land reform had begun. The record on civil liberties was a very good one.

The military dictatorship that overthrew the Allende regime has been highly repressive. Headed by Augusto Pinochet, it has relied on military rather than political strategies for strength. Poverty and class struggle remain facts of life in the country. Unfortunately, army rule has not been a prelude to the return of the Christian Democrats. Today Chile can be described as a graveyard of dreams. Hundreds of persons have been arrested without witnesses, taken off the streets never to appear again.

General Pinochet has announced the end of "liberal democracy," since it was too weak and incapable of controlling Marxism.[8] He expresses contempt for persons who play into the hands of the "international Communist conspiracy" through their concern for the human rights of a few. His own interest, he proclaims, is the rights of all Chileans. Pinochet describes his new democracy as "a clear, solid, and rigorous doctrine that emanates from the juridical bases of the Chilean institutional system."[9] In fact, the executive, legislative, and judiciary are joined together in the military, leaving civil liberties without meaning or defense.

Pinochet takes as models not only General Franco of Spain but also Diego Portales, the early nineteenth-century strong man of his own country.[10] Portales put a stop to revolution and created a centralized Chile. In the end, however, his militarism was self-defeating. One morning when he came out to review his troops, he was forced to kneel down and was shot.

Characteristically, Pinochet has warned the Roman Catholic church about its activities. Separated from the state since 1925, it remains in touch with the workers. It feeds tens of thousands of persons daily, defends the imprisoned, and tries to discover the whereabouts of missing persons.

The development of Latin American military dictatorships has been studied carefully by Professor Juan J. Linz, a political scientist at Yale University.[11] Linz distinguishes two patterns. One attempts the controlled mobilization of a population not previously mobilized. Perón in Argentina is an example of this type. The regime in Chile seeks the reverse: the demobilization of the masses, thus reducing popular political participation. Such a strategy appears when institutions have not guaranteed a stable base for change or satisfied the demands created by mobilization. In his research, Linz has given special attention to Brazil. He points out that in this country neither the old ruling classes nor the new left have been strong enough to resist dictatorship. Linz describes it as having an authoritarian situation but not a fully authoritarian regime. He makes this distinction to emphasize that a completely totalitarian condition has not been effected.

The Military in Brazil

The military regime in Brazil continues to employ arbitrary arrest, torture, and terror promiscuously. Terror on the left has been largely suppressed. From the right, it persists uncontrolled. The President is said to be opposed by some of his own generals when he attempts to repress violence. Instability in the armed forces is evident from frequent "institutional acts" and changes in the election laws and the constitution. The churches, students, and intellectuals continue to protest.

In the past, the military has sometimes been a fourth force, replacing the monarchy as a kind of stabilizing and regulatory agency.[12] It has intervened before and then withdrawn. However, this time it has remained in power since 1964 and has produced no popular leader. The industrialization sought through dictatorship has brought little rise in actual living standards for the masses. The political enemy remains indefinite and only vaguely identified: urban terrorism or communism. Late in 1967, General Moniz de Aragao renewed the anti-Communist campaign. Accusing the Roman Catholic church of helping subversive groups, he included among the latter virtually all unauthorized opposition.[13]

In 1978, Brazil's fifth consecutive military president is scheduled to be chosen for a six-year term. Technically, he will be voted into office by an electoral college of the Congress. The real choice will be made by the four-star generals of the high command. At mid-summer, 1977, Brazilian newspapers and magazines were inundated with a flood of information about the career of a particular military officer. His family life and background became public knowledge. There were reports of how he goes horseback riding in Brasilia, the capital, after dawn each morning except Sunday, descriptions of how he spent his youth, and how he still enjoys solving difficult mathematical problems. The general's picture appeared on the cover of virtually every major magazine. The publicity was all part of an unofficial "primary" campaign for the presidency.

Political Parties

Presidents may come and go, but unrest will not cease until some popular base is established and cultural pluralism is acknowledged. Only two parties have been allowed in Brazil: ARENA, the Alliance for National Renewal; and MDB, the Democratic Movement of Brazil.[14] During an election campaign, a candidate may appear on radio and television and tell his name, profession, and party. However, he cannot speak to such issues as inflation, the decline in real income, pollution of the environment, health, the right to work, or political prisoners. In protest, a large part of the electorate abstains from voting.

In November, 1974, the MDB, the opposition party, apparently won the majority of votes in an election. However, no change came about. The president can rule by decree without Congress. At his behest, its members may have their mandate taken away or lose immunity from arrest. Many politicians have had their political rights taken away.

It is important to recognize that the United States' stand is very important, since Latin American military regimes are highly conscious of their foreign image. They continue to need outside capital and technology. Politically, the models they can adopt are limited: the Communist totalitarian state, the republican model, or fascist dictatorship.[15]

Today, imponderables remain. The Roman Catholic church, intellectuals, and workers could change the balance of power. When Linz wrote his study on Brazil, he did not anticipate that all General Franco had stood for would so soon be renounced.[16]

The Press

In Brazil, censorship has a legal basis in the 1967 constitution. Section IV, Number 8 states that everyone has a right to free expression of his opinions and political convictions or world view, as well as a right to information without censorship.[17] However, a legal exception is made for public meetings and assemblies. Books, newspapers, or magazines are not allowed to "undermine public order." Brazilian courts have ruled that publishers and journalists can be arrested and penalized for breach of these provisions. In fact, police squads are physically present to watch over newspaper presses.

Some limited "decompression" was hoped for when President General Ernesto Geisel came to power in 1974. However, the only positive change that followed was that the censor functioned more promptly from the capital city. Texts sent by air to Brasilia on Monday are returned Tuesday evening. Photographs and quotations must be included. Certain people are not allowed to be mentioned by name. Newspapers cannot report police action in the country. For a brief period in January, 1975, they were allowed to publish lists of persons who had disappeared and were sought by friends or relatives. This is no longer the case.

Not only political and economic debate is forbidden; cultural life is also restricted. Literature, music, and the arts suffer. The mood is one of fear and self-censorship as well as repression. In a single year, more than one hundred theatre plays and sixty films were forbidden.[18] Two hundred musical titles remained unplayed. Every forty-eight hours a book was forbidden. The restrictions imposed on Chico Buarque de Holanda—the popular singer, composer, and writer—are typical. More than one hundred thousand of his records have been sold. He is well known and accepted. Yet only an hour before one of his concerts, the program was subjected to censorship.

Discussion of major questions of national importance is thwarted. For example, the magazine *Movimento* undertook a nationwide survey of the place of women in Brazil, enlisting eighty-two journalists, sixty-three of them women.[19] Its data showed that the six million working women on the average received less pay than men. Two million of them were employed in households, one million in the fields. But the facts could not be discussed publicly. The censor forbade 283 of *Movimento*'s 305 columns, 58 of 69 photographs, and 10 of 12 tables.

The most outrageous violation of human rights in the area of communication is the torture and murder of journalists. In October, 1975, the police reported that Vladimir Herzog had taken his own life at the torture center at San Paulo. Colleagues do not believe the story. One of them, Rodolfo Osvaldo Konder, was impounded with Herzog but not killed. At the torture center he was told that Herzog was a KGB Communist agent. In reality the murdered man had an international reputation for integrity and worked for the BBC.[20]

Argentina

The unhappy legacy of Perónism in Argentina, a rich land with a high literacy rate, continues today. Jeane Kirkpatrick, in a careful study published by the MIT Press, shows how limited violence was institutionalized under this populist dictator.[21] Before his death, Perón was again arresting his enemies. A kind of lower-class Caesar who appealed to the masses, he twice turned his country into economic shambles. It was part of Perón's political strategy to use the labor unions against an older, established class oligarchy; they remain an important force in Argentina today. Perón limited but did not destroy the freedom of the press. "It should serve the truth," he said. Perón restricted individual liberty but instituted no single-party ideology. Although purging the judiciary, he established no centrally controlled totalitarian institution.

Provincial, direct, and crude, Perón was hardly a Buenos Aires sophisticate. His popular appeal was enhanced by his mistress, Eva, who subsequently became his wife. Illegitimate by birth, traditional standards would have kept her in obscurity. Yet she became a symbol with whom the urban poor identified. Perón's populism inhibited Marxism from spreading among the working class as much as in some other Latin American countries. Neither was the working class as lost to religion. Perón reinstituted religious instruction in state schools, and for a period he was supported by the Roman Catholic church. Perón was finally thrown out by the army, assisted by the church and the older established classes. Chaos remained, however. From 1955 to 1966 alone, Argentina had five different presidents—two military and three civilian.

Hector Campora's candidacy in the 1973 presidential election was used as a front for Perón's return. In September, 1973, Perón himself received 60 percent of the popular vote. His career exemplifies the way in which human rights in Argentina have suffered through the failure of both populism and military rule. Argentina has been led by authoritarian figures throughout most of its history; Perón was only one among many, but he was a colorful character. His strategy was to encourage mass political activity but not decision-making. In reality, he enlisted mass participation for policies that were unsuccessful. Corruption was not arrested. By the time Perón died in July, 1974, the inflation rate had reached 335 percent.

His second wife, María Estela Martinez de Perón, succeeded him. Before the end of the year she declared a state of emergency. Three thousand persons were arrested for subversion. A death squadron sponsored by the social ministry is credited with at least 1,500 murders.[22] Left-wing organizations have replied in kind. The Montoneros take their name from the nineteenth-century Gaucho rebellion, and ERP, Ejército Revolucionario del Pueblo, has a Trotskyite orientation.

After Perón

The junta of General Jorge Videla overthrew Mrs. Perón in a military putsch on March 24, 1976, promising to control the terror. Videla said he intended to kill every guerilla. But in fact, in the next three months there were three times as many political murders as before. Journalists, lawyers, politicians, professors, writers, and artists have all been victims. The unofficial execution of persons held under arrest is defended by the allegation that they have attempted to flee. A special mission of Amnesty International sent to the country confirmed that prisoners have been kept from water, food, and sleep.[23] It found that torture in Argentina includes electric shock, water treatment, beatings, burning with cigarettes, cold baths, the use of wild dogs, and sexual abuse of women.

José Comblin, a political scientist, observes that the ideology of national security competes with democracy in South America.[24] It was expressed in General de Meira Mattos's book, *Brasil, Geopolitico e Destino,* published before Secretary of State Kissinger went to Brazil.[25] General Golbery de Couto e Silva of Brazil writes, "The nation is absolute or nothing. A nation can accept no limitations of its absolute power."[26] Chile's Major Claudio Lopez Silva argues, "The Third World's armed forces are the only social organization that is cohesive, capable, and efficient enough to cope with the socioeconomic problems of the underdeveloped countries."[27]

A strategy used in emergency situations threatens to become permanent. It is, in fact, totalitarian, and is intended to shape all facets of national life—economics, culture, politics, even population control. As in the case of Nazism, the state is viewed as the supreme "organism" that the people must serve; ideology is anti-Communist. Comblin believes the denial of the democratic tradition has derived from three fundamental concepts: geopolitics, total strategy, and the privileged role of the armed forces—state = power = security. A state dominating a center of geographical space possesses a will and purpose of its own which enables it to act independently of persons. It must grow, struggle, expand, and defend itself. Every state is involved in unremitting war. There is no difference between civilian and soldier; all are participants.

National Security Ideology

The ideology of national security justifies permanent authoritarian governmental structures. Rule by decree extends emergency powers indefinitely. Massive arrests include not only avowed leftist revolutionaries and politicians, but anyone suspected of sympathizing with them—labor leaders, journalists, university professors, and students. Refugees from political oppression cannot escape by seeking exile in a neighboring land. A computer bank in Chile collects information on political opponents for six countries.[28]

The secret police, Brazil's SNI and Chile's DINA, enforce order.[29] A supreme cabinet or council of state is made up of the heads of the military branches and occasionally a few civilians. It oversees the entire political, social, economic, and cultural process, and appoints the president of the republic. Legislatures, when tolerated as in Brazil, are reduced to passive roles. The judiciary is impotent. In fact, the attack on religion is not radically different from that of communism. The military attempts to turn the entire community into an armed forces camp, controlling and exploiting organized religion.

According to Comblin, such regimes recognize the effectiveness of Christian symbolism in mobilizing the masses against Marxism. "Religion is an indispensable factor in the psycho-social strategy." Purely personal faith does not matter, but traditional practice based on accepted symbols of

Christianity is valued. National security regimes generally wish to cooperate with the church, up to a point. The state will guarantee the church status and give it privileges. Organized religion in return will enlist the masses in an anti-Marxist campaign.

Whereas national security regimes are interested superficially in traditional symbolism, Christianity is concerned with people. Roman Catholics and Protestants alike have been forced to a more courageous defense of human liberty and democracy. There is less and less legacy from the nineteenth century, when the Roman Catholic Church was reluctant to accept the liberties proclaimed by the French Revolution. Official policy has changed, especially since Pope John XXIII's *Pacem in Terris*. Christ's word is to be accepted personally. Experiencing the abuse of political power leads to renewed consciousness of the self as a free person before God. Christians have become the voice of the voiceless so that persons will learn to become persons again.

In actuality, national security state strategies are anti-people. They lead to the economic, social, and political manipulation of citizens, transforming them into an alienated mass. In the Christian view, human rights are not derived from the citizenship granted by the state. New birth in Christ makes new people. The church is not the distributor of traditional symbols and spiritual consumption goods as national security regimes wish; it is the people of God, expressing His judgment and love.

9

The State vs. Religion in Eastern Europe

The Russian party newspaper, *Izvestia*, published the full text of the Helsinki Conference agreement in its February 8, 1975, edition. Article VII reads, in part:

Respecting human rights and basic freedoms, including freedom of thought, conscience, religion, or conviction: the participating nations will respect human rights, including freedom of thought, conscience, religion, or conviction for all persons without distinction regarding race, sex, language, or religion. They will support and encourage the effective exercise of civil, political, economic, social, cultural, as well as other rights, all of which derive from man's intrinsic dignity and are essential for his free and full development. In this area the participating nations will recognize and respect the freedom of the individual alone or with others, to profess and practice a religion or conviction in accordance with the dictates of his conscience.[1]

In June, 1977, a week before the opening of the Belgrade Conference, which was to review the observance of the Helsinki accord, 635 religious leaders from 107 countries in Africa, Europe, the Americas, and Asia were invited to Moscow by the Orthodox Patriarch. The head of the Russian Orthodox church convoked the large conference on the theme "Religious men in favor of lasting peace, disarmament, and just relations between nations." His guests included Jews, Christians, Hindus, Muslims, and Buddhists. Some who attended described the occasion like something out of a storybook, a lavish occasion with hospitality comparable to that shown foreign officials.

Soviet Premier Alexi Kosygin made the opening address. In honor of the invited guests, the Moscow Orchestra and Chorus staged a three-hour program, half of which was devoted to Russian religious music. Prime television time was given to reports of the meeting, and its appeal for disarmament and peace was made known worldwide: "We do not speak from a position of power but appeal with affection and consideration for humanity. War and military preparations are contrary to the spiritual world order and undermine the fundamental moral rights of man."[2]

The question of human rights in Russia itself could not be avoided. Pastor Gaillard of France described civil and personal liberties as the most pressing issue in Russia, even as he acknowledged socialist concern for social justice. One member of the conference observed, "On balance, I would say that when anything like this happens in the USSR, the government must be convinced that there is something in it for them."

What was the Soviet purpose? Was it a search for support in important sectors of domestic and foreign opinion? The fact is that religion continues in the USSR today. Repression is not complete, as it is in China or Albania. The Soviet government seeks to control religion and to use it for state purposes. But persecution has not ceased.

A Letter to the Patriarch

From Alexander Argentov, 21 July 1976.
To his Holiness Pimen, Patriarch of Moscow and of all Russia.
Your Holiness, I turn to you as head of the Russian Orthodox Church with a request for help.

On July 14 of this year I was taken by force to the psychiatric hospital, although I was without symptoms of mental illness. As the doctors said openly, the only reason for my admittance was my belief in God and membership in the Orthodox Church.

I am healthy and I sleep excellently, but here I am given strong sedatives. I am by nature mentally well-balanced and quiet, but here I am forced to take Anninasin, supposedly to calm me, and I am threatened with forced injections if I refuse.

Here I am placed among violent patients who must be tied to their beds. . . . But what still depresses me more is the doctors' attitude; although completely ignorant in matters concerning religion, they try to convince me that my religious belief is a mental sickness. They say that our Christian belief prevents us from defending the fatherland, that the progress of aeronautics and the cosmonauts' flights prove that there is no God, that priests serve only for money, and that young believers are mostly psychopathic idiots. Although my parents are militant atheists, they recognize that I am well and have repeatedly tried to have me released from the insane asylum.[3]

Aksenov, a *samizdat* commentator, describes the tragedy of the larger situation: "An indecisive episcopacy pretends not to realize that the government's representative for religious affairs removes worthy priests who are respected by the people from parishes, only to replace them with drinkers and mercenaries."[4]

Father Dudko

That is what happened to Father Dudko, confessor of Solzhenitsyn. Removed from the parish of St. Nicholas in Moscow, he was subsequently put under the authority of a collaborator priest. More recently he has been physically attacked on the street. Dudko baptized more than 5,000 adults. He conducted question-and-answer sessions while at St. Nicholas. Large numbers attended the sessions, which lasted from six to ten in the evening.

The priest spoke simply. A believer asked why there are so

many religions. Dudko replied, "Because we are sinners and we are in error. As soon as we are in error, each of us seeks an exit, but each in his own way. There is only one exit: that which leads to God. To seek God is always good; not to believe is evil. Who boasts in his own faith is not a believer. Who does not appreciate his own faith is not near to God. For us, Orthodoxy is the right faith. But when there will be no more sin, then there will also be only one faith. Christianity must become the content of the entire life. Christianity ought to shed light on all problems. It cannot remain closed within a framework. . . . It is necessary to 'ecclesify' all of that part of life which is conducted outside the walls of the Christian temple. Much depends on this 'ecclesification.' "[5]

In fact, the alienation that existed between the church and the intelligentsia before the revolution has been overcome. It is young people and intellectuals who are most interested in religion in Russia today.

Someone asks Dudko, "How do you explain youth's interest in religion?"

Dudko answers: "It is the soul that thirsts for God. Persecution only accelerates the religious process. As we know, the center of the religious process is the cross. They crucified Him and received the opposite in return: not death but resurrection."

The priest asks a group of young people, ages twenty-four to thirty, "What made you be baptized?"

"We do not really know," comes the answer, "but we have understood that Christianity is the world we lack."

Communist Policy

The year after the Helsinki agreement, the publishers of the Great Soviet Encyclopedia asked Vice Chairman Furin of the Council of Religious Affairs to lecture for them. His remarks on the state of religion in the Soviet Union received publicity beyond the range of his hearers.[6] Furin asserted that the general tendency in Russia is for religion to decline and become extinct. He reported that in 1975 only 19 percent of all children were baptized, whereas in 1965 the figure was 30 percent. Forty percent of funerals are religious, but believers account for just 10 to 15 percent of the urban population and 20 to 25 percent of the rural inhabitants.

Orthodox churches have been decimated since the revolution, from 77,676 to 7,500. In the Baltic states, only about 1,000 of almost 4,200 Roman Catholic churches remain. Formerly there were 24,000 mosques. Only 1,000 remain open, with only 300 registered. The number of Orthodox priests is not being maintained. Although there are two candidates for every seminary vacancy, the selection board rejects the majority of those applying for reasons of health or because they are "possessed by religion." The Council of Religious Affairs, Vice Chairman Furin reported, works to strengthen legality in church-state relations and to straighten out "voluntarists" in local areas. Of the 16,000 congregations of sects in the country, only 60 percent are regarded as loyal to the regime. Estimates are that 1,200 congregations remain unregistered and illegal.

State Supremacy

Soviet policy dates from the time of Lenin, who insisted that the Communist party could not allow religion to remain a simply private matter. Continuing opposition to faith in God is based on laws that date from Stalin's terror; most of them have been on the statute books since 1929. Bibles are not available. Religious education of children and youth is forbidden.

The campaign against "religious obscurantism" was initiated while Lenin was still alive. Stalin thought he had come close to extinguishing the church before World War II. However, this was not the case. He was forced to moderate his attack under the pressure of hostilities during the war.

Some respite continued until the time of Khrushchev, when the antireligious campaign was renewed. Nearly half of the Orthodox churches still open in the country were closed. Officially, separation of church and state is proclaimed. Actually, the regime attempts to control religion by registration and restrict it to the sanctuary.

The Soviet Council of Religious Affairs reports to the USSR Council of Ministers. One of its chief responsibilities is the strict observance of Soviet law. Groups dependent on a priesthood (for example, the Orthodox) are in some respects easier to regulate than the low-church groups (for example, the Baptists). For Baptists, it is not enough to close sanctuaries and defrock the clergy; they must be further restricted—if possible, through their own officials.

The state seeks to dominate and control all types of religious leadership. A group of Baptists, insisting on full separation of church and state, withdrew from the officially authorized Baptist body in 1961. Their leaders have been hunted down and arrested. The issue of survival vs. martyrdom is not a simple one. Baptists and other believers who cooperate with the regime should not simply be condemned as collaborators. Persons allowed to go abroad for meetings must have positive relations with the government. Their outside contacts help keep religion alive.

On the surface, the Russian bureaucracy resists pressure. In fact, it is sensitive to world opinion and has yielded in small measure to international protests.

Helsinki

Believers who continue to practice **their** religion in the USSR—Jews, Christians, Buddhists, **and** Moslems—had hoped that restrictive measures directed against them would be lifted following the Helsinki accord. Even though this hope has not been fulfilled, the Helsinki Conference is appealed to.

It would be naive to dismiss their protests simply as anti-Communist or anti-Russian propaganda, as government sources charge. Anatolij Levitin-Krasnov, now living in exile in Switzerland, has written in detail about conditions under the renewed antireligious campaign.[7] Levitin-Krasnov believes it was the intent of Stalin to discredit clergy by forcing them to work with and for the state. Khrushchev attacked more directly, invoking nuclear technology and space travel as apologetics for atheism.

An example of this is Levitin-Krasnov's personal experience. He was a teacher in School 116 in Moscow. One day the director of the school called him into his office. The government press had carried reports of material written by a public schoolteacher defending belief in God. "Are you that teacher?" the director asked. The answer was affirmative, and Levitin-Krasnov had to give up a vocation he had pursued with integrity since he was nineteen.

What happened was that the dismissed school teacher realized the USSR does not practice religious neutrality or encourage pluralism. It is an ideological regime dedicated to the propagation of godlessness and the ultimate destruction of religion, even though it allows some religious leaders a limited exercise of their function in the sanctuary. Different convictions do not compete openly in the marketplace. Religious publication or freedom of church organization is not allowed.

Levitin-Krasnov decided to answer a particularly blatant atheistic book that had been published as part of the renewed antireligious campaign. In only two weeks he assembled his material in typed copies. Metropolitan Nikolai, who received one of them, remarked, "This is really serious writing."

Levitin-Krasnov points out that there was a vigorous intellectual discussion of the meaning of Christianity even amid persecution. He wrote from 1961 to 1967 for the *samizdat* magazine *En Route*, helping to fill the vacuum of Christian apologetics. He cites as examples of scholarly studies the history of religion written by Alexander Men: volume one on the history of ancient China and India; volume two on ancient Egypt, Babylon, and Buddhism; volume three on antiquity; volume four on the Bible; and volume five on Perfection: the Son of Man.

Conversion

The issue is not just intellectual but personal. *Samizdat* underground writings carry not only theological discussions, but describe authentic conversions to Christ.[8] However, Christianity is not accepted without reflection. Christian rebirth brings spiritual renewal and change. Experience of the Christ of the cross is reported in testimonies that recall the Acts of the Apostles and the first Christian centuries. *Samizdat* writings emphasize that conversion means conquering the "pathos of immanence"—the belief that some available event will save the world. This aspect of Marxist utopianism is the root of totalitarian conviction and makes it most dangerous.

Christian experience is the antithesis of such totalitarian control and the violence it employs. In Christian terms, violence is always harmful because of its inherent consequences. It disfigures and kills men, ruining society and rendering vain every elevated goal in the name of which it is practiced. At the same time, it is recognized that personal responsibility must come with this condemnation. Psychological violence and the slogans and jargon of the triumphalistic high-sounding phrases of the official Soviet press belong to the same pattern. Christians under persecution come to recognize their personal responsibility to reject it. They find freedom, community, and the courage to criticize from their own personal experience of grace.

Ideocracy

Nelidov is probably a pseudonym for a recent convert from atheism to Orthodox Christianity.[9] His writings seem to show wide experience. Nelidov begins his commentary by saying, "A revolution carried out in order to free from oppression and exploitation led to the autodivinization of the state, in which it became possible to canonize every form of slavery and exploitation." He continues further, "This form of slavery was destined to repeat both to itself and to its own subjects that the society in which they live is the most free, advanced, and flourishing. The state imposes not only itself by force, but by an abstract idea whose pretext is to be accepted by the human conscience without discussion."

Nelidov uses the term "ideocracy" to describe the incredible masquerade in which ideological marionettes are substituted for real humans. Society becomes an impersonal, formless mass, leveled out by a gigantic ideological steam roller. Ideocracy, he believes, keeps men in the state of children. It is as if they were educated in an orphanage by a neutral and impersonal administration.

Samizdat authors, including non-Christians, often argue that society is even more sick in spirit than in its structures. Nelidov's interpretation is that "the absolute dictator was not Stalin, but rather a divinized truth which mysteriously possessed men." What happened was that "everyone's conscience was deformed by a strange optimism in regard to humanity and by savage instincts in regard to the concrete human person."

"Here an incredible mythical system was born," writes Nelidov. "The individual lives in a world wherein contact with reality comes about only through the mediation of certain ready-made phrases (or slogans). The reality behind these slogans remains for all practical purposes unknown; still impulses generated by the myth act on the individual."

Christian *samizdat* recognizes that the masses, indifferent and apathetic, are passively integrated into the system. Fearful and timid, they are either tranquilly atheistic or superstitious. The consequence is schizophrenic dichotomy of the spirit, a double character of the person which expresses itself at best in stupidity, at worst in cynicism. "The stupid" still remain simple consumers of ideology. The greatest evil of such a system is not external oppression but the renouncing of one's own personality. The disease of the society takes root in a person and corrupts his heart. Nelidov writes in conclusion, "The ideological conscience presupposes a renunciation of liberty; where one does not know what to make of his liberty, liberty is considered disorder and shameful."

Spirit

Spiritual awakening, however, is spoken of even beyond the Christian circle in Russia. Apathy is challenged. Vol'nyj writes, "The difference between this rebirth and the Renaissance of the fourteenth century is that the latter proceeded from the Spirit to Man, whereas that of today proceeds from man to spirit." The question is not one of "forgetting man to take refuge in the spirit, but rather of consolidating man *in* the spirit."[10]

Such a spiritual revival is understood as necessary to defend persons from the abuse of power, to conquer fear, indifference, and falsehood. Change of socioeconomic structures is not enough. Man the concrete individual becomes the center of attention. A new focus on common human bonds grows out of a sense of the supreme value of spirit which is within man but greater than him. Nelidov writes, "The struggle for the liberation and dignity of the human person is being conducted out of a firm awareness and testimony that man is a spiritual being, and that this spirituality is the source of his liberty and dignity. In touching clay, the spirit creates man; only the spirit makes man."

Sragin, an agnostic, writes, "It is precisely the spirituality of the opposition that creates its real force, even in inexpressible concrete terms. The regime encounters this as though it were a wall, each time it tries to eliminate it."[11]

But this kind of spirituality does not attempt to withdraw, as did some types of pre-revolutionary Russian idealism. Rather, accepting the world as God's creation, it strives to embrace everything. The Russian experience of communism has produced an awareness that a change of structures often only modifies the facade and is mere appearance when it is unaccompanied by renewal.

The Legend of the Grand Inquisitor

Concern for the relation between freedom and spirituality is deep in the Russian tradition. The basic issue was elucidated by Dostoevski in his novel *The Brothers Karamazov* in the last century.[12] His insights expressed in the legend of the Grand Inquisitor were tragically prophetic. They apply not to Roman Catholicism—which Dostoevski misunderstood and misrepresented—but to communism in Russia today.

Dostoevski's story is set in Seville, Spain, during the most terrible time of the Inquisition. Jesus came down into the hot streets and lanes of the city. He appeared quietly, inconspicuously, but everyone recognized Him. The people were drawn to Him by an irresistible force; they surrounded Him, thronged about Him, and followed Him. Jesus healed a blind man who asked His help. On the steps of the cathedral He raised a little girl from the dead. The Grand Inquisitor, passing by, ordered Jesus' arrest. The crowd immediately made way for the guards and a deathlike hush descended upon the square.

The prisoner was taken to the dark, narrow, vaulted prison of the Inquisition. Day passed and was followed by the dark, hot, "breathless" night of Seville. Then the iron door of the prison opened suddenly and the Inquisitor himself entered slowly. "Is it You, You?" he asked, but receiving no answer he added quickly, "Do not answer; be silent. And indeed, what can you say? I know too well what you would say. Besides, you have no right to add anything to what you have said already in the days of old. Why then did you come to meddle with us? Was it not you who said so often in those days, 'I shall make you free'? . . . For fifteen centuries we have been troubled by this freedom, but now it is over and done with for good."

The Grand Inquisitor spoke of Jesus' first temptation: "If thou be the Son of God, turn these stones into bread." Jesus refused any discipleship bought by loaves of bread. But the Inquisitor argued that this was the only possible way. There is nothing more alluring to man than freedom of conscience, but there is nothing more tormenting either, the Inquisitor urged. Human creatures fear and dread freedom. In their innate lawlessness, they cannot even comprehend it.

Nothing has ever been more unendurable to individuals or society. In the end, men will lay their freedom at the feet of those strong enough to endure it—the few like the Inquisitor—and say, "We don't mind being your slaves so long as you feed us." A tranquil mind and even death is dearer to man than free choice in the knowledge of good and evil, the Inquisitor believed. Instead of taking possession of man's freedom, he concluded, Jesus multiplied it and burdened the spiritual kingdom of man with its sufferings forever.

The chief concern of these miserable creatures, the Inquisitor believed, was to find something they all believed in and could worship. The absolutely essential thing was that they should all do so together. Therefore, they had persecuted and tortured others of different beliefs. And so it will be to the end of the world even when the gods have vanished from the earth. Men will prostrate themselves before idols in just the same way.

After the Inquisitor finished speaking, he waited for some time for Jesus' reply. The silence distressed him. Jesus kissed the old man on his bloodless, aged lips. The Inquisitor gave a start and then went to the door and opened it. "Go, and come no more," he said. "Don't come at all—never, never." And the prisoner went away.

But freedom, just as questions about freedom, does not go away any more than the need for it goes away. The Inquisition is now in the hands of the pagan state, which continues to make itself absolute.

10

Human Rights—
Past and Future

I. The Contemporary Crisis

The crisis of human rights needs to be seen in its historical background. Two world wars in the first half of the twentieth century were indescribably terrible in their impact on human life. The world was not made safe for democracy as Americans had hoped. Instead, a whole civilization seemed to collapse in a return to barbarism, and with it respect for human rights. In the longer perspective, it is clear that hatred and destruction in World War I were the precursors to totalitarianism.

The hostilities of World War II ended with the dropping of two atomic bombs on Japan, beginning a new age of nuclear threat and terror. The full nihilistic potentialities of the present era still cannot be assessed. Will civilization endure? When and where will the arms race end? Science and technology have reached their highest levels of development. But at the same time, they bring unparalleled apocalyptic possibilities of sudden annihilation, mass suffering, and degradation. The post-Helsinki debate about human rights comes amid uncertainties of an uneasy peace between superpowers.

The competition between nations has taken on new and unpredictable dimensions; so, too, has man's inhumanity to

139

man. Human rights has become more important than ever in such a situation. Earlier, the abuse of human rights, as terrible as it was, had limited geographical scope. Today, the possibilities of oppression are worldwide. Hitler practiced genocide against a whole people, and Nazism became a threat to all mankind. Adopted by a highly educated people in a scientifically advanced, sophisticated society, it made a mockery of moral traditions.

Hitler was defeated, but Stalin's successors use psychiatry and work camps to perpetuate tyranny. The old Russian empire of the Tsars had long practiced repression and the persecution of minorities. Yet as Solzhenitsyn has shown, its murders were few compared to the paranoid terror of Stalin's purges. "Brainwashing" had already begun in his show trials. The topography of his Gulag Archipelago has been described even by French Communists as a kind of descent into hell.[1] Unlike Dante's inferno, its tortures have been real and not imagined.

Two world wars exemplify the kind of human depravity in which whole eras can be caught up. The desire of rulers to perpetuate themselves in office overcomes considerations of justice. Absolutizing their own ideologies and wishes, they disregard human rights. It is easier to imprison or even to murder citizens than to grant them minimal freedom and fight poverty.

Fate and Freedom in History

The present crisis has its basis in decisions made over the past decades. In the longer view, one can observe impersonal forces mixed with personal initiative and freedom. History is not simply impersonal—as is physics—or organic—as is biology. This was evident in the pattern of two world wars. Great movements—militarism, nationalism, technology, and the drive for self-determination—were reflected in these events. At the same time, they were also shaped by the decisions of individuals: an assassin's determination to kill the heir to the Austro-Hungarian throne, the reaction of the emperor in Vienna as well as other heads of state, the decision of Woodrow Wilson to involve the United States in World War I. In the era of World War II, larger historical forces conditioned the careers of Chamberlain, Churchill, and Roosevelt as well as Hitler and Stalin. But policies and their implementations turned on the leaders' responses.

The face of human rights in the future will continue to depend on such a combination of men and movements. Little if anything is "automatic." Human beings must still make decisions in freedom. A world grown small is increasingly interdependent economically and socially as well as politically. Nation states continue to assert their sovereignty without qualification. Yet few if any nations have resources to live independently; even great powers seek allies in self-defense. New technology can enhance the power of the secret police. At the same time, the urge for personal liberty grows.

The status quo was altered radically by two world wars. The world is now divided between East and West, North and South. Superpower engagement is part of our political and economic era, dictated by geography as well as history. The United States attempted to live in isolation even after World War I; it was forced decisively into a world power role in 1941 at Pearl Harbor. Stalin tried to divide Europe with Hitler until his own country was attacked. Today, his successors do not want to give up the power base achieved at the close of hostilities. Yet in terms of the threat of warfare, Washington and Moscow are closer now than Paris and Berlin in the last centuries.

Politics and government have been viewed passively by the majority of human beings most of the time. Many believe that whatever are the forces that shape the institutions of human life, they are too large to be controlled or even influenced effectively. It is often thought that government is not an appropriate object for moral judgment. Politics is not ruled by moral standards, but rather by the law of the jungle. At least, it is not subject to the norms of personal relations, even though it may have its own code of honor. Professor William Lee Miller concludes, "Most of the world has believed in some mixture of these things about its collective life. On the whole Americans have not. Apparently, Jimmy Carter does not."[2] Carter's stance has been one of activism and idealism; it, too, belongs to the history of the era.

Carter's Achievement

Anthony Lewis, during several weeks in Western Europe, asked foreign policy professionals and government leaders about President Carter's human rights policy.[3] Lewis tried conscientiously to canvass their views without bias, more than half a year after Carter had come to office. Lewis reported that each person he interviewed mentioned problems that could be raised. "But without exception they have praised the policy as a whole, and most of them have spoken of it with an enthusiasm unusual in established governmental figures." Lewis explains the reason for the favorable view, using the words of a diplomat in London with no time for illusions. "At first I reacted with professional skepticism. I worried about jeopardizing relations with the Soviet Union. I worried about raising expectations too high. . . ." The diplomat admitted that now he is ashamed of the way he felt. Questions must be asked. "But I have come to see that Carter **is** raising a standard to which the wise and honest can **repair** again in America." He concluded that Carter has made human rights a part—a useful part—of the diplomatic dialogue over a very wide area.

Respect for basic human rights has been eroded not only by totalitarian oppression but by cynicism and skepticism. In all events, human rights have only a relative claim, it is said. Power is the only resort; might alone makes right. Rights are not granted by God; they are established by civilization or the state. Carter does not share this view, not only because he is a Christian, but because he believes in the American political tradition. Recognition of standards of justice and a sense of human fairness does not resolve all difficulties. But it does make possible a more responsible approach.

One need not be personally religious, much less a Baptist Christian, to understand the relevance of human rights. Yet it would be a mistake to discount the fact that Carter's dedication to human rights is rooted in biblical religion and the teachings of Jesus. In the face of oppression, liberty is championed most of all by those who believe in it as an absolute moral obligation. Carter's faith conveys a sense of the absolute, but it is in a context of judgment and radical forgiveness. He has emphasized that criticism of human rights violations applies to his own nation as much as to others. Christianity works against self-righteous rationalization. It demands personal renewal in the name of righteousness. Professor Miller cites C. Vann Woodward's claim that the heritage of the South is far more closely in line with the common lot of mankind than the national legends of opulence, success, and innocence.[4]

Christian Realism

It is a mistake to regard Carter as a naive idealist, projecting some absolutistic moral pattern on the world. Rather, Christian conviction leads him to accept the world for what it is, with all its good and evil. He knows the biblical warning against pride. The world passes away. Political action is relative. Salvation comes from God, not politics. The Christian can accept a variety of ways to reach his goal because he knows things are ultimately in order. Proximate strategies do not mean an amoral policy; discussion, negotiation, and compromise are necessary. In a world with goods and evils, struggle against injustice is necessary. The politician expects self-interest, selfishness, and sin, but he need not despair. A naive secularism all too easily fails to understand why a Christian religious view is more inclusive and adequate.

Urban political reporters get sweaty trying to interpret Carter. Set against present-day political criteria, he may be a mystery. But in the light of older cultural and moral values, he represents the central legend of his culture—the active will mastering the environment. This is the conclusion of one of his most perceptive interpreters.[5] The basic moral substratum of American culture was preserved under the crust of the South, even as it was eaten away elsewhere by the acids of modernity. Carter believes in purposeful action upon the external world, improving life for one's neighbor. He refuses to accept the prospect of an inferior life for anyone. Miller acknowledges that there may be something perilous in the return of the world-fixer, the moralist, the Puritan, or the evangelical with an "interfering spirit of righteousness." But the promise is much greater than the potential drawbacks.

Natural Rights

Doctrines of natural rights were developed in the eighteenth century under the influence of the Enlightenment. As Marx pointed out, the age of feudalism was followed by that of an absolute monarchy and, in time, by the rule of the middle class. Natural rights were said to come from the word of the Creator. Liberty, regarded as a God-given right, was joined optimistically with equality and fraternity. Enlightenment claims were in part a secular version of the Christian vision of a perfect society, but without its awareness of evil.[6] The dominant rationalism embraced an optimism about human nature that has been destroyed in the era of two world wars.

Critics have pointed out, retrospectively, that natural rights were recognized in response to particular needs and problems. For example, representative democracy grew up in the struggle against absolute monarchy and the fight for freedom from arbitrary interference by the king and the established church. This observation, however, does not resolve the issue of their universal truth and value.

In Anglo-Saxon countries, a certain consensus about the necessity of human rights is still honored. However, it cannot be taken for granted worldwide. If rights are to have reality, they must be more than just statements on paper. Today, the pressure of events has made clear that respect for civil liberties is dependent on common traditions and beliefs. The form of a government is secondary to its commitment to liberty. Respect for personal dignity can be expressed in a variety of organizational structures. A fundamental belief about man and history is what matters. The present crisis arises most of all from the fact that the underlying bases of accepted rights have come into question.

One commonly argued thesis is heard less frequently than before in the face of contemporary totalitarianism. The claim was that increased secularization had led to a growth in human rights. Today the reality of tyranny raises questions of ultimate meaning. How long will the present crisis last? Will a civilization emerge that affirms the freedom and dignity of persons? Or will there only be the cynicism and impotence that has come in the wake of two world wars? A positive understanding of human rights is called for in the face of nihilism; their denial is in effect the death of the spirit.

Creation, Redemption, and Eschatology

Fundamentally, the Hebrew-Christian perspective is threefold; it is based on the themes of creation, redemption from sin, and eschatology. Creation means that man is made by God in His own image and is intended to have fellowship with Him. Human life is not a lucky accident; it has an intrinsic value and meaning established by God. People are not just biological phenomena or means to political ends. On the contrary, concern for their freedom and welfare is divinely commanded.

According to the Bible, God is not merely a force or idea but an eternal being with a righteous will, personally active and concerned for individuals. Grace awakens man to the possibilities of fellowship with God. Christianity may renew civilization ethically through concern for personal worth and dignity. But this is not its primary purpose. Redemption is not concerned simply with freedom from temporal tyranny, but with liberation from sin and death. It is concerned not only with time but with eternity. The biblical view is not naively optimistic: Man is sinful, selfish, and idolatrous. On the other hand, new birth has been made possible through Jesus Christ.

During the election campaign, reporter Kandy Stroud visited Jimmy Carter's Sunday School class.[7] She concluded that he meant what he said there. He was not just looking for a winning issue, as in political debate, nor was he seeking compromise. The Sunday School lesson really did matter for him personally. On the day of Mrs. Stroud's visit, the lesson concerned Christ's return to earth. The point that was made was a familiar one, at least for those who attend Sunday School regularly. A Christian should live as if the end of the present age could come at any moment, being ready for the "last things."

This theme of eschatology—the study of "last things"—can be illustrated from Carter's reflection. What can such a concern have to do with the presidency of the United States? Indeed, could it not interfere with responsible political judgments? In reality, the end of all human life on the planet is a possibility the president of the United States must reckon with as he holds responsibility in an age of potential nuclear warfare. Eschatology has this secular dimension, however its religious meaning is appraised today. That the early church's expectation was not immediately fulfilled by no means destroys eschatology's relevance—concern for life after death and moral judgment. As the fourth Gospel makes clear, eschatology embodies a fundamental view of reality and personal life which Carter accepts.

Historians of religion point out that primitive man's world view is not linear but cyclical. It looks to a golden age in the past, and through ritual attempts to recapture its power and meaning.[8] Primitive men live in fear of time, seeking to escape from its perils. Their religion was based on the nature cycle rather than history, an outlook which has continued even into some of the more developed religions. Biblical faith embodies a radical break with this cyclical view; it is future-oriented and "linear." Hope is no longer just in the past, but in what can be through the providence of God. The Bible deals with evil and its defeat in history. Its message is one of a God who forgives and redeems and is concerned for persons.

Reinhold Niebuhr, the theologian Carter refers to often, has emphasized the profundity of Christian eschatology compared to less complex views of history.[9] More than just a temporal sequence is involved: God's providence is understood to bring a moral imperative. Niebuhr emphasizes that Jesus' Sermon on the Mount has an eschatological setting, radically expressing the demands of God's pure will. The Sermon on the Mount tells how life will be when the kingdom of God comes. The kingdom is not simply an individual, private matter, but also has a social reality that concerns human rights. In the words of the Lord's Prayer, it means that God's will is done on earth even as it is in heaven.

The Christian promise of a new age requires respect for individuals of all classes. Men cannot be treated ruthlessly, not because they have merit by themselves, but because God cares about them. Active love of neighbor is enjoined for

God's sake. The Christian is to seek righteousness in a sinful world. It is not only man's concern, but God's also. Carter's Bible-oriented, low-church personal piety is not an escape from the world. At the same time that it affirms the separation of church and state on New Testament grounds, it also requires participation in public life.

II. Human Rights in History

The U.S. pattern has been one of freedom *for* rather than freedom *from* religion. Separation of church and state does not imply atheism or agnosticism. The crisis of human rights is clarified if one accepts that neither national nor international politics is devoid of religious meaning. Religion in this sense is not just a confessional matter; it includes self-understanding and a judgment of reality.

The defense of human rights in the United States has its roots in Puritanism and low-church tradition as well as in the Enlightenment. The American pattern of checks and balances drew more heavily on religious realism than rationalistic optimism. Aware of the arrogance of power and having resisted absolute rulers, Americans instituted a republican form of government that refused to give unqualified authority to any single official. Protestantism was dominant in the United States until the latter half of the nineteenth century. The sense of human equality and respect for the duties of citizenship has Reformation religious bases. Roman Catholic and Jewish elements were subsequently included in the American synthesis with the arrival of new immigrants. The Roman Catholic outlook has a sense of human solidarity— even as it shows an understanding of the perennial character of evil. The acceptance of tolerance and pluralism at the Second Vatican Council was influenced by the American experience.

Four Traditions

When the United Nations was founded, Professor James T. Shotwell of Columbia University wrote to the U.S. Secretary of State, calling attention to the problems of human rights. His letter led to the U.N. commission that drew up the 1948 declaration. Professor Shotwell's volume, *The Long Way to Freedom*, is a historical study of the growth of human rights from primitive to contemporary societies.[10] Shotwell's study shows that modern human-rights doctrines have at least four identifiable sources: Greek democracy, Judeo-Christian religion, modern science, and the Puritan and Enlightenment beliefs in reason and freedom.

Greek Democracy

Greek philosophy developed objective moral bases for the rule of law. Plato was shocked by the execution of the man he considered the greatest and best—his model and teacher, Socrates. Partly as a result of his revulsion over Socrates' execution, respect for human rights has become a part of the Greek philosophical legacy. At the same time that Socrates recognized the authority of the state, his first obedience was to a higher law. To be sure, he took the institution of slavery for granted, as did Plato and Aristotle. For them, human rights was limited to the freeman.

Democracy, a legacy from the Greek city-state, carried with it a sense of the rights and duties of citizenship. The principles of liberty and justice were considered grounded in the nature of the universe and reality. The case is explicit in Plato's *Republic* as well as Aristotle's *Politics*.[11] Although Greek democracy declined with the rise of the empire, its insights were preserved in Roman law and in Christian interpretation. Athens was admired in the Reformation and the Renaissance as well as in the Middle Ages.

Hebrew-Christian Faith

The faith of the Hebrew prophets remained unique. Earlier, the defeat of a nation in warfare caused the demise of its gods and acceptance of those of its conquerors. By contrast, the biblical prophets proclaimed the justice and righteousness of a God whose sovereignty was not circumscribed by the nation's destiny. He could send His own chosen people into captivity for their sins, but would in time also restore and deliver them. In short, Amos, Hosea, Isaiah, Jeremiah, and Ezekiel taught that the covenant with their God did not give His people unqualified divine sanction or blessing regardless of their actions. Prophetic faith was not a rationalization for the status quo but a judgment against it. It refutes the Marxist claim that religion is an opiate of the people.

Christians shared the Hebrew prophets' conviction that man and the state are responsible to God and His law. At first a persecuted minority, they were forced to assume individual responsibility. Affirming freedom of conscience, they proclaimed an inner personal revolution: "We ought to obey God rather than men."[12] The early Christians did not reject government. However, they refused to worship the Roman emperor as divine, and for this reason they were persecuted to the death.

The revolutionary character of their affirmation is not to be underestimated. Christian claims are universal, not limited by race or tribe. Human beings are to be respected, not just because they are persons, but because God Himself cares about them. Liberty is God's purpose for man. It was not Greek philosophy but Judaism and Christianity that taught the intrinsic dignity of all men.

Modern Science

After the Emperor Constantine ended the persecution of the Christian church, the church joined with the monarchy in a union of throne and altar. Mediating the Greek and biblical legacies, it often worked for the rule of law. However, established religion also persecuted others. Modern science's need for human rights is exemplified by Galileo's resisting the Inquisition. His idea of the universe was broader than that of his opponents. Like Sir Isaac Newton, discoverer of the law of gravity, Galileo reflected on the order and wonder of God's creation. For him, the laws of nature could not be explained simply materialistically. Nor ought the freedom to explore them be circumscribed.

Modern science has provided new critical bases for knowledge which have challenged intolerance and bigotry. It is mistaken to claim, as did Marx, that science is simply materialistic. Rather, in its attempt to discover the pattern of the universe, modern science is a work of freedom and personal integrity. It depends on human creativity and insight. More than technology, it suffers setbacks when personal liberty is denied. Such has been the case even today under communism.

Puritan and Enlightenment Beliefs

In modern political traditions, human rights have been established by three revolutions: the Puritan, which took place in England during the seventeenth century, and the American and French revolutions in the late eighteenth century. In *The Long Way to Freedom*, Professor Shotwell argues that the human rights accepted in the Glorious Revolution of 1688 in England have their basis in Puritanism. They had been championed by spokesmen like Milton and Cromwell. Shotwell cites Cromwell's address to his Second Parliament: "Fundamentals are somewhat like a Magna Carta, which should be standing, be unalterable. . . . Liberty of conscience is a natural right, and he that would have it ought to give it."[13]

Government of the people, by the people, and for the

people embraces the Puritan denial of the divine right of kings or any authoritarian party. Legitimate rulers come to office through legal elections. They are responsible to the people, taking office with the authority set forth in basic documents that identify the nature and limits of government.

There was no real parallel to this type of religious criticism of government in the French Revolution. The Huguenots had been dispersed by persecution. Unlike the French pattern, the American Revolution had no Robespierre bringing a reign of terror. There was also no return to imperialism under a Napoleon.

The achievement of separation of church and state in the U.S. cannot be ignored in the history of human rights. Freedom of conscience came to be accepted under the influence of the Enlightenment and free-church traditions. Rhode Island has been described as the first modern state that guaranteed full religious liberty and separation of religious matters from civil authority. Its founder, Roger Williams, insisted that government can never assume the role of God, who alone is Lord of conscience. Genuine faith must be free and voluntary. Williams argued for the equality of all persons and groups before the law.

Professor Perry Miller of Harvard University wrote of Williams:

> For the subsequent history of what became the United States, Roger Williams possesses one indubitable importance, that he stands at the beginning of it . . . as a figure and a reputation he was always there to remind Americans that no other conclusion than absolute religious freedom was feasible in this society.[14]

Human rights claimed in the American Revolution were compromised drastically by slavery for nearly a century. The new nation conquered a continent. It was an open country protected by two oceans, and its sense of national destiny continued even through a bloody civil war. Now, the age of innocence has passed. Clearly it is not possible to return to an earlier isolation; issues have become worldwide. The problems of world order, economics, natural resources, terrorism, nationalism, and disarmament bear in on the great powers. New ideology and technology have emerged. The United States has a very different ethos now than when it was a rural land with a frontier. Human rights require state protection in urban America. Racial desegregation and integration have come only after World War II. An irresponsibile individualism is as unnegotiable as a collectivistic totalitarianism.

Conviction

"We Americans are waffling between God's blue sky and the Red Devil on the issue of human rights. It's time to face the issues,"[15] observed Carl F.H. Henry, an outspoken Protestant theologian. He notes that the American Declaration of Independence identifies the divine Creator as the transcendent source and sanction of human rights. "To a radically secular society, this may seem to be a bit of quaint poetry." Nonetheless, the fact remains "that the insistence of the classic American political documents on a transcendent source and sanction of human rights (whether it was ventured on theistic or deistic principles or both we need not argue here) is of immense importance."[16]

Such analysis has the virtue of posing clear alternatives. The argument is that both theistic and deistic doctrines of human rights have been displaced by evolutionary naturalism. European naturalism—Marxism, for example—has been ruthless. American naturalism, like Dewey's "common faith," held a larger respect for human rights. Can it give hope for the future?

"Given evolutionary emergence, no reason exists why a superman, as Nietzsche held, or a superspecies, as Hitler thought, might not appear in the wide spectrum of humanity." In fact, such a view can offer no objective values. "The loss of God as the source, sanction, and stipulator of human rights befogs the precise identification of human rights."[17] Bertrand Russell asserted rightly that there is no reason for attaching finality to man on a simply evolutionary premise.[18] Still higher forms, to whom man as he currently exists would be as insignificant as the primal protozoa, can appear. In short, naturalism cannot account for value or human dignity; nor is its evolutionary optimism adequate to the fact of evil. It ought not be invoked as a substitute for faith in God.

Hitler

More than thirty years after the death of Adolph Hitler, a German motion picture attempted to explain and evaluate his life.[19] Some commentators felt that his only fault had been that he made political mistakes. "If he had died just after the Munich Conference," they remarked, "he would have been regarded as a great statesman who did much for Germany." Other viewers observed that Hitler's urge to conquer the world would not have been satisfied until it brought victory or destruction. The latter viewpoint raises the fundamental moral question of the purposes and limits of the state. Nazism embodied an explicit rejection of the moral and religious bases of human rights.

Hitler honored the nineteenth-century philosopher Friedrich Nietzsche and in fact erected a shrine to him. Whether Nietzsche would have been a Nazi is dubious. Hitler was correct, however, in recognizing a rejection of Christianity and its value in contempt for the common man. Nietzsche, more than Hitler, understood the terror which comes with "the death of God." He recognized the crisis a civilization undergoes when its basic values are reduced to impotence by disbelief. In its full dimensions, the crisis of human rights is a religious one. Nietzsche's "Madman" cries out:

> Whither is God? I shall tell you. We have killed him—you and I. All of us are his murderers. But how have we done this? How were we able to drink up the sea? Who gave us the sponge to wipe away the entire horizon? What did we do when we unchained this earth from its sun? Whither is it moving now? Whither are we moving now? Away from all suns? Are we not plunging continually? Backward, sideward, in all directions? Is there any up or down left? Are we not straying as through an infinite nothing? Do we not feel the breath of empty space? Has it not become colder? Is not night and more night coming on all the while?[20]

Paradoxically, the answer to Nietzche's claims about the death of God comes from a Russian—Dostoevski. Nietzsche knew of his writings but chose to avoid any detailed reading of them. Dostoevski, having probed atheism to its limits, linked religion and freedom.

The Future

Christians, like Marxists, seek to identify the scope and direction of history. What will the world be like in 1984 or 2000? Will life be more humane and decent, with greater fulfillment for individuals? Or will it be increasingly chaotic, distressed, and oppressive? English historian H. G. Wells once spoke of an imaginary time machine. It would enable a person to go backward or forward through time a decade or a century or a millenium. Who has the courage to ask what the world will be like in ten years or at the end of the century? Will the planet be terrorized, poverty still widespread, natural resources exhausted? What will be the state of human rights? Of course there are other concerns: peace, economics, social welfare, environmental control, and world order. Yet the defense of liberty in the face of repression must be a high priority. Personal integrity is at stake. What is done in the present will significantly determine the future.

The totalitarian state characteristically seeks to eliminate opposition. Russian psychiatrists who coerce dissidents have been divided into a variety of types. The Philistine is intent on survival and a comfortable living at all costs, and is dangerous to dissidents for obvious reasons. The writer of dissertations can sometimes be counted on for support; he can adjust the definition of mental illness, making it broad or flexible enough to permit the state to have its way in dealing with a dissident. Or, the novice, eager to flex his diagnostic muscles, may be prepared to call almost anyone sick. Characters who are ready to be service instruments of the powers that be no matter what the nature of the request can only be described as professional hangmen. They abuse human rights out of a lack of respect for persons. Social reform is stifled. For them, there are no absolutes. Such an outlook means the end of all hope for the future. Christian concern for human rights challenges this abuse of fellow men.

Threefold Pattern

It is not necessary to invoke religion to establish the fundamental need for human rights. Yet the fact is that in the modern world religion has been increasingly a defender of freedom. Christianity's role and influence need to be appreciated in relation to the threefold theme that has emerged in Eastern Europe amid persecution: motivation, clarification, and prophetic criticism.[21]

The Christian commitment to human rights provides motivation at the deepest level. The struggle is rooted in God's will that men should be persons. Fellow men are to be accepted and respected, treated justly, and loved for God's sake. Anything else is sin.

The clarification and "unlocking" of human rights is also a Christian obligation. Ideology and propaganda need to be demythologized. High religion not only refuses any simplistic black-and-white judgment, but it requires self-criticism before God's righteousness. All too easily, rights are made into a rationalization for a given political order. What is called for is not uncritical affirmation of the beliefs of a particular place or era, but careful, critical discernment.

The prophetic view of human rights is found in both the Old and New Testaments. God's righteousness requires concern for the poor and oppressed and is set against all injustice. Rights are not just negative—such as protection of personal liberty—but are effected positively through community responsibility and service. Institutions as well as persons need to be reformed again and again.

Defense of Liberty

By their very nature, human beings seek hope for the future. Their actions follow from what they really believe. Both Marxism and Christianity offer a horizon of hope—not only a new age, but ultimate fulfillment. Despair is countered by a vision of what ought to be. The thesis of this book is that only a religious defense of human rights is adequate in the world of the future. Naturalisms such as Marxism in the end fail to do justice to the dignity of man. Belief in an absolute does have a positive effect.

Michael Polanyi, a Hungarian biologist and philosopher who lived in the West, understood religion's role in the defense of liberty. Before his death, he called attention to "inconsistency" in the intellectual foundations of the modern frame of mind in Western culture.[22] Polanyi warned that inconsistency could even lead to the destruction of our civilization. At the same time that the impact of modern science on our concept of knowledge has led to a critical philosophical positivism that is dubious of the reality of moral motives, a

157

skeptical sophistication tends to view morality as a high-sounding rationalization for lesser but truer motives. This makes it easier to take a denunciatory rather than an affirmatory form. Nevertheless, a social and political dynamic remains, which is in part a secular version of Christian moral fervor. Fundamental demands for the perfection of man continue even when their religious basis dissolves.

Polanyi acknowledges that a combination of skepticism and moral denunciation has led to many reforms that have humanized Western society. Yet presently it tends to debilitate any positive defense of the values of Western civilization. Any intellectual who attempts to argue that moral goodwill has been an effective force in Western civilization runs the risk of being dismissed as naive and unscientific. Polanyi concludes that a society in this frame of mind expresses its desire for progress mainly in an attack on itself. The efficacy of goodwill is attributed to class interest. The field is left open to cynical accounts that undermine moral confidence in the past and future direction. This is the issue in the human rights debate.

The defense of human rights does bring results. Today, they came to the prisoner and told him he was free. He could return to his family. Why? The reason was no more evident than it had been for his arrest. Had political conditions changed, not just nationally but internationally? Someone cared and spoke out with power. One can never be fully sure why dictatorial regimes release some prisoners of conscience.

Not all of his fellow prisoners were freed. There was still oppression in the land. But human life had greater possibilities of being what its Creator intended it to be. This is what human rights means.

Notes

Chapter 1

1. *Time*, March 7, 1977, p. 2.
2. Otto Frederich Nolde, *Freedom's Charter, The Universal Declaration of Human Rights* (New York: Foreign Policy Association, 1949), pp. 55-62.
3. *Argentinien Bericht einer Mission von November 1976* (Vienna: Amnesty International, 1977), p. 39.
4. *Christian Science Monitor* (European edition), July 18, 1977.
5. Ludmilla Thorne, "Inside Russia," New York *Times* Magazine, June 12, 1977, pp. 26ff.
6. *London Times*, September 2, 1977, 1A.
7. *Encounter*, Vol. 47, No. 6, June, 1977, p. 92.
8. Ibid., p. 92.
9. Ibid., p. 92.
10. Denis Goulet, "Prolegomena to a Policy, Thinking about Human Rights," *Christianity and Crisis*, 37:8, May 16, 1977, pp. 100ff.
11. Maurice Cranston, "Human Rights, Real and Supposed," in D. D. Raphael, ed., *Political Theory and the Rights of Man* (Bloomington: Indiana University Press, 1967), p. 53.
12. Vernon van Dyke, *Human Rights, the United States, and World Community* (New York: Oxford University Press, 1970), p. 73.
13. *Time*, April 11, 1977, pp. 12, 19.
14. New York *Times*, March 2, 1977, p. 4.
15. *Nation*, April 1, 1977, p. 389.
16. *Time*, March 28, 1977, p. 25.
17. Thomas Griffith, who writes occasional commentary for the *Atlantic Monthly* and *Time*, has spoken in this vein.
18. Samuel Decalo, *Coups and Army Rule in Africa* (New Haven: Yale University Press, 1976), pp. 5ff.

19. Goulet, "Prolegomena."

20. Ibid.

21. Jacques Maritain, *Man and the State* (Chicago: University of Chicago Press, 1951).

Chapter 2

1. See Lincoln P. Bloomfield, *In Search of American Foreign Policy* (New York: Oxford University Press, 1974), pp. 64-74.

2. David Berg and George Feifer, *Solzhenitsyn* (London: Hodder & Stoughton, 1972), p. 229.

3. Irving Howe, "A Word for the Dissidents," *Dissent*, Spring, 1977, p. 115.

4. New York *Times*, July 10, 1977, sec. 4, p. 2.

5. Ibid.

6. *Religion und Atheismus in der UdSSR*, No. 3, March, 1977, p. 116.

7. Leonard Schroeter, *The Last Exodus* (New York: Universe Books, 1974), p. 302.

8. Ibid., p. 306.

9. Ibid., p. 307.

10. New York *Times* Magazine, June 12, 1977, pp. 26ff.

11. *Glaube in der 2 Welt*, No. 13, 1977, D. 18.

12. London *Times*, May 10, 1977, p. 1C.

13. *The Listener*, June 16, 1977, pp. 768-70.

14. New York *Times*, February 3, 1977, p. 33.

15. *Encounter*, Vol. 48, No. 5, May, 1977, pp. 83-85.

16. Ibid.

Chapter 3

1. Peter Millard, *Prager Winter* (Vienna: Herold, 1977).

2. Michael Cockerell, "Chartists of Eastern Europe," *The Listener*, June 16, 1977, pp. 766-67.

3. Ibid., p. 767.

4. Ibid.

5. *New York Review of Books*, August 4, 1977, pp. 11-15.

6. Ibid.

7. "Terror in Czechoslovakia," *Spectator*, May 7, 1977, pp. 7-9.

8. Trevor Beeson, *Discretion and Valor* (Glasgow: Collins, 1974), pp. 190ff.

9. Ibid.

10. Thorne, "Inside Russia," pp. 26ff.

11. Raymond Aron, *Uber die Freiheit* (Frankfurt: Fischer, 1968).

12. *Hungarian Review*, December, 1976.

13. See "Polen: Die Kirche und die Intellektuellen," *Wiener Tagebuch*, No. 7/8, July-August, 1977, pp. 40-41.

14. Erik-Machale Bader, "Totenklage im Karnevals Kontraste in Krakow," *Frankfurter Allgemeine Zeitung*, No. 114, May 17, 1977, p. 3.

15. *Spiegel*, No. 22, 1977, pp. 111-12.

16. Testimony by Gustaw Herling-Grudzinski before U.S. Congressional Commission on Security and Cooperation, New York *Times*, June 8, 1977, p. A 21.

17. Ibid.

18. *Spiegel*, No. 22, 1977, pp. 111-12.

19. "Polen," *Wiener Tagebuch*.

20. *Spiegel*, No. 35, 1977, p. 124.

21. London *Times*, October 10, 1977, pp. 4f.

Chapter 4

1. *Time*, February 28, 1977, p. 30.

2. James M. Perry, "God's Grace and a Little Guile," *National Observer*, March 26, 1977.

3. Elizabeth Drew, "A Reporter at Large: Human Rights," *The New Yorker*, July 18, 1977, pp. 36ff.

4. *Newsweek*, June 20, 1977, p. 53.

5. Ibid., p. 54.

6. *Time*, January 31, 1977, p. 10.

7. New York *Times* Magazine, July 3, 1977, pp. 16ff..

8. Drew, "Reporter at Large," pp. 36ff.

9. Michael Reisman, *Nation*, May 7, 1977, pp. 554-55.

10. *Presidential Documents*, Vol. 13, No. 12, p. 401.

11. New York *Times* Magazine, July 3, 1977, pp. 16ff.

12. Perry, "God's Grace."

13. Van Dyke, *Human Rights*, pp. 130-41.

14. Brzezinski, *Between Two Ages* (New York: Viking Press, 1970).

15. Cf. *Foreign Policy*, Summer 1976, pp. 65-96.

16. Ibid.

17. Brzezinski, *Between Two Ages*, p. 24.
18. Harvey Shapiro, "A Conversation with Jimmy Carter," New York *Times*, Book Review, June 19, 1977, pp. 1ff.
19. Ibid.
20. Perry, "God's Grace."
21. *Christian Century*, April 20, 1977, p. 372.
22. Perry, "God's Grace."
23. *New York Review*, May 12, 1977, pp. 16ff.
24. New York *Times*, May 23, 1977, p. 12.
25. *Christian Science Monitor* (European edition), June 13, 1977, p. 30.
26. *Encounter*, Vol. 47, No. 6, June 1977, pp. 30-39.

Chapter 5

1. They include Jean-Marie Benoist, André Glucksmann, and Bernard-Henri Lévy.
2. Wolfgang Leonard, *Three Faces of Marxism* (New York: Holt, Rinehart and Winston, 1974), p. 51.
3. Ibid.
4. Ibid., p. 47.
5. John Reed, *Ten Days that Shook the World* (New York: Boni and Liveright, 1919), pp. 125-26.
6. *The Christian Science Monitor*, November 1, 1977.
7. "Greetings to the Hungarian Workers," May 27, 1919, *Works*, XXIX, p. 391.
8. *Rosa Luxemburg Speaks* (New York: Pathfinder Press, 1970), p. 389.
9. "Debatte über die Pressfreiheit," *Rheinische Zeitung*, May 5, 1842, *Works*, I, p. 54.
10. Ibid.
11. Ibid.
12. Preface to *Critique of a Political Economy*, January, 1859. Cf. *Marx and Engels Selected Works*, Moscow, I, p. 503.
13. Robert Tucker, *Philosophy and Myth in Karl Marx* (Cambridge: Cambridge University Press, 1961).
14. Khrushchev, "The Crimes of the Stalin Era," in Boris I. Nikolaevsky, *New Leader*, 1962, pp. 12-13.
15. Karel Kosik, "The Crisis of our Time," *Literarni Listy*, No. 7-12, 1968.

16. *Rude Pravo*, April 10, 1968.
17. *Die Zeit*, No. 29, July 8, 1977, p. 2.
18. Ibid.
19. *Time*, June 20, 1977, p. 49.
20. Franz Marek, "Eurokommunisten und Bürgerrechtskämpfer," *Wiener Tagebuch*, Vol. 6, 1977.
21. Ibid.
22. *Oesterreichische Monatshefte*, No. 5, 1977, pp. 29-30.
23. Marek, *Wiener Tagebuch*.
24. Ibid.
25. Ibid.
26. Leonhard, *Three Faces*, p. 277.
27. Ibid.
28. Joachim Nawrocki, "Die Relativierung der Menschenrechte," *Osteuropa Archiv*.
29. Leonhard, p. 306.
30. Ibid.
31. Rudolf Bahro, *Die Alternative, Zur Kritik des real existierenden Socialismus* (Cologne: Europäische Verlag, 1977). Cf. *Spiegel*, No. 35, 1977, pp. 30-40.

Chapter 6

1. *Time*, June 27, 1977, p. 16.
2. *Africa Report*, May-June, 1976, p. 4.
3. Ibid., November, 1976, p. 2.
4. Ibid., January-February, 1977, p. 2.
5. Ibid., p. 3.
6. Heribert Adam, *Modernizing South Africa's Racial Domination, South Africa's Political Dynamics* (Berkeley: University of California Press, 1971), pp. 37-40.
7. Ibid., pp. 23ff.
8. Ibid., pp. 53ff.
9. J.C. Davies, "The Circumstances and Causes of Revolution," *Journal of Conflict Resolution*, 11, 3:255.
10. Peter Walshe, "The U.S. and Southern Africa," *Commonweal*, April 1, 1977, p. 201.
11. *Africa Report*, May-June, 1976, p. 20.
12. *The Wall Street Journal*, June 22, 1977.
13. *Time*, March 17, 1977, pp. 19ff.

14. Decalo, *Coups and Army Rule*, p. 1.

15. Ibid., pp. 220ff.

16. Reported by the Council of Churches on International Affairs, N.Y. Meeting of March 21, 1973.

17. Cléophas Kamitatu, *La Grande Mystification du Congo-Kisnishasha*, p. 12.

18. *Time*, February 28, 1977, p. 31.

19. New York *Times*, July 20, 1977, p. A 19.

Chapter 7

1. Arthur Macy Cox, *The Dynamics of Détente: How to End the Arms Race* (New York: Norton, 1976), p. 212.

2. "The Terrifying Prospect," *Atlantic Monthly,* April, 1977, p. 62.

3. Ibid., p. 53.

4. Ibid., p. 57.

5. Ibid., p. 63.

6. *Presidential Documents*, Vol. 13, No. 12, p. 360.

7. Bloomfield, *In Search of American Foreign Policy,* p. 148.

8. Ibid., p. 146.

9. Cited in Cox, *Dynamics of Détente*, p. 212.

10. *Presidential Documents*, Vol. 13, No. 12, p. 397, 399.

11. New York *Times*, May 11, 1977.

12. Cox, *Dynamics of Détente*, p. 222.

13. *Time*, April 11, 1977, p. 21.

14. *Time*, March 21, 1977, p. 28.

15. Cox, *Dynamics of Détente, p. 213*.

16. Alexander Solzhenitsyn, *August 1914* (New York: Farrar & Straus, 1972).

17. Alexander Solzhenitsyn, *Lenin in Zurich* (London: Bodley Head, 1976).

18. "World Development and U.S. Foreign Policy: The Opportunity Before Us," June 10, 1977.

Chapter 8

1. *IDOC Bulletin*, Rome, No. 1, 1977, p. 8.

2. Georges-André Fiechter, *Brazil Since 1964: Modernization Under a Military Regime*, tr. Alan Braley (New York: Wiley, 1975), p. 144.

3. Ibid., p. 144.

4. Ibid., p. 146.

5. Ibid., p. 147.

6. Ibid., p. 3.

7. Richard O'Mara, "Studies in Government by Terror," *Saturday Review of Literature*, April 2, 1977, pp. 12ff.

8. Ibid.

9. Ibid.

10. Ibid.

11. Juan J. Linz, "The Future of an Authoritarian Situation or the Institutionalization of an Authoritarian Regime, the Case of Brazil," in Stephen Alfred, *Authoritarian Brazil's Origins, Policies and Future* (New Haven: Yale University Press, 1973), pp. 233ff.

12. Fiechter, *Brazil Since 1964*, p. 23.

13. Ibid., p. 136.

14. Ibid., p. 186.

15. Ibid.

16. Linz, "The Case of Brazil."

17. *Zensur in Brazilien* (Cologne: Amnesty International, 1976).

18. Ibid.

19. Ibid.

20. Ibid.

21. *Leader and Vanguard in Mass Society, A Study of Peronist Argentina* (Cambridge: MIT Press, 1971).

22. *Argentinien: Bericht einer Mission von November 1976* (Vienna: Amnesty International, 1977), p. 8.

23. Ibid., pp. 47ff.

24. *IDOC Bulletin*, Rome, No. 1, 1977, pp. 2-8.

25. Ibid., p. 7.

26. Ibid., p. 3.

27. Ibid., p. 4.

28. Ibid.

29. Ibid.

Chapter 9

1. *Religion und Atheismus in der UdSSR*, No. 22, July-September, 1976, p. 20.

2. *Christian Science Monitor* (European edition), June 27, 1977.

3. Reported in *Glaube in der 2 Welt*.

4. "Society and Church in the Soviet Union," by a representative of *Russia Christiana* (Milan), Driebergen Congress on the Church in Eastern Europe, Interacademical Institute for Missiological and Ecumenical Research, Utrecht, p. 13.

5. Ibid.

6. *A Chronicle of Human Rights in the USSR*, No. 22, July-September, 1976, p. 20.

7. Anatolij Levitin-Krasnov now writes for *Glaube in der 2 Welt*.

8. "Society and Church in the Soviet Union," p. 12.

9. Ibid., p. 7.

10. Ibid., p. 9.

11. Ibid.

12. *The Brothers Karamazov*, book 5, chapt. 5.

Chapter 10

1. *Time*, September 12, 1977, pp. 29-30.

2. New York *Times* Magazine, July 3, 1977.

3. New York *Herald Tribune* (International Edition), June 24, 1977, p. 6.

4. New York *Times* Magazine, July 3, 1977.

5. Ibid.

6. Carl Becker, *The Heavenly City of Eighteenth Century Philosophers* (New Haven: Yale University Press, 1932).

7. Kandy Stroud, *How Jimmy Won* (New York: Morrow, 1977), p. 162.

8. Mircea Eliade, *Cosmos and History* (New York: Harper, 1959).

9. Reinhold Niebuhr, *Nature and Destiny of Man* (New York: Scribners, 1943).

10. James T. Shotwell, *The Long Way to Freedom* (Indianapolis: Bobbs-Merrill, 1960).

11. Ibid., pp. 101ff.

12. Acts 5:29.

13. Shotwell, *Freedom*, p. 335.

14. Perry Miller, *Roger Williams: His Contribution to the American Tradition* (Indianapolis: Bobbs-Merrill, 1953), p. 254.

15. Carl F.H. Henry, *Christianity Today*, July 8, 1977, p. 25.

16. Ibid.
17. Ibid.
18. Ibid.
19. *Spiegel*, No. 34, 1977, pp. 62-63.
20. Cf. Karl Jaspers, *Nietzsche* (Tuscon: University of Arizona Press, 1965), p. 242.
21. Gunter Krusche, "Menschenrechte in Theologischer Perspektive, Eine Gesprachsbeitrag aus der DDR," unpublished, IDOC files, Rome.
22. Cf. Thomas A. Langford, *Intellect and Hope, Essays in the Thought of Michael Polanyi* (Durham, North Carolina: Duke University Press, 1968).